Le Corbuffet

Edible Art and Design Classics
Esther Choi

Prestel
Munich • London • New York

CONTENTS

Introduction

Sometimes the universe sends you hints and nudges in the form of unexpected gifts. In 2014, I found myself sitting in a concrete bunker, sorting through a passel of paper. My August days had been spent in archives, searching, painfully, for clues. Research for my doctorate degree in architectural history had taken me to unexpected places. That week in East Anglia was no exception.

So, imagine my amazement, monotony interrupted, when I discovered an elaborate menu. Designed by the Hungarian artist László Moholy-Nagy, the multi-panel bill of fare was for a dinner in honor of Walter Gropius, the famed German modernist architect and Bauhaus school founder.

László Moholy-Nagy
Farewell Dinner for Gropius, 1937

Gropius and his family were about to leave London. Like other European modernist architects in 1937, he and his family had been living in exile, avoiding Nazi occupation, narrowly escaping a fate that many others did not. He'd accepted a prestigious job at the Harvard Graduate School of Design. The event marked both an end and a beginning: the conclusion of a period of uncertainty and transience, and the start of yet another chapter of life as immigrants in a foreign country.

I began to see Gropius in a new light. In the way that food can operate as an index of social status, cultural taste, lifestyle, and class privilege, it allowed me to render a different portrait of a man, deemed a genius by most art and design textbooks. As much as the menu revealed the cultural assimilation required of the Gropiuses to survive in England and the United States, it also brought their immense privilege into plain view. Britain's intellectual and artistic glitterati partook in a glamorous evening of gastronomic indulgences that night—far from the typical diet of the average person during a period of interwar rations.

This strange and beautiful artifact led me to realize that food performs in particularly unique ways, revealing aspects of our society and its structures through subtler means. Certainly, its relatively low cost and accessibility have made it a preferred medium for artists and designers engaged in social and cultural commentary. To the artist-run SoHo restaurant FOOD, devised by Carol Goodden, Tina Girouard, and Gordon Matta-Clark in the early 1970s;

Richard Landry, with alteration
by Gordon Matta-Clark
Food, 1971

to feminist collective Womanhouse's immersive domestic installation of a dining room in 1972; to Haus-Rucker-Co's edible architectural models for their *Food City*

Beth Bachenheimer, Sherry Brody, Karen
LeCocq, Robin Mitchell, Miriam Schapiro,
and Faith Wilding
Womanhouse: Dining Room, 1972

events, also in the early 1970s; to, more recently, Rirkrit Tiravanija's pad thai served to museum and gallery goers (*Untitled*, 1990), food has prompted new ways to understand, and challenge, the place of aesthetics in the politics of everyday life.

Lodged within the quotidian rituals of commensality are profound questions about the nature of human existence. Consider, for example, Alison Knowles's Fluxus performance, *The Identical Lunch* (1969–), in which the artist visited the same luncheonette in Chelsea, New York, at the same time, and ordered the same daily spread: a tuna fish sandwich on wheat toast, with lettuce and butter (no mayo); and a large glass of buttermilk or a cup of soup. She came to think of the lunch as a performance and published an event score. Reenacted by others, the range of experiences produced by the same meal revealed the work's main philosophical gambit: no object in human experience is identical to itself.

Likewise, the rituals of food consumption reveal that we are the same, but different. Alike, but also unlike. We all must eat in order to survive. Yet how and what one eats is anything but universal. As much as food can magnetize relations, it is also a seismograph of privilege. Some have easy access to an abundant and stable food supply. For others, access is severely limited, associated with scarcity and toil. Walk into any average grocery store and you can tell a lot about a neighborhood's demographics. What vegetables, or fruit, if any, are available, and how much do they cost?

Art and design function in this way, too. As modes of creative production that can question and dismantle barriers, they can also effectively produce and reinforce them through their participation in privatized channels of market value and art fairs, which limit access. Gropius, like many modernist designers, touted the democratic values of making good products available for the masses. Yet their designs are now stored away in museums and private collections, embalmed by the market's insatiable desire for aesthetic consumption. While creative expression was once regarded as an activity as natural as eating, in today's economy, commensality and aesthetic connoisseurship are becoming increasingly rarefied and inaccessible endeavors, subject to the social systems and institutions that separate the haves from the have-nots.

In 2015, I decided to conduct a social experiment. Inspired by the menu for Gropius's dinner, I wondered: If I re-created this bill of fare for my friends, would I come closer to reconciling the aspirations of the avant-garde artists and designers I so admired, in relation to the circumstances that afforded them their place in it? I envisioned my circle of confidants, arms in the air. With irony, we'd wear monastic cloaks inspired by Johannes Itten, while toasting merrily with glasses of Tio Pepe. Yet I had to face the facts: No one, in this day and age, wants to eat turtle soup, nor could I bring myself to actually de-shell a terrapin and boil it.

Still, refusing to be dissuaded, I dreamt up a scenario to defuse some of the pretense surrounding the gastronomic and artistic cognoscenti. In April 2015, I organized my first *Le Corbuffet*—a domestic food situation named, cheekily, with a feminist wink, after the famed modernist and notoriously misogynistic French architect Le Corbusier. I developed a series of pun-inspired dishes named after canonical works of art and design. An invitation was sent to twenty people, summoning them to my tiny Brooklyn apartment.

Esther Choi
Invitation for *Le Corbuffet*, April 2015

The first event featured a number of dishes included in this compendium. My friends gobbled up plates of Carolee Schneemann *Meat Joy* Balls, an orgy of juicy, spiced, aromatic lamb kefta piled high over mounds of couscous and roasted vegetables. They marveled over the frank, conceptual boldness of a platter of Lawrence Weiners, naked, boiled, and unapologetically unadorned. Mouthfuls of a Michael Heizer *Levitated Mass* Pavlova were enjoyed between giggles, its geological meringue peaks slathered in clouds of whipped cream.

As a culinary and artistic celebration of satire, *Le Corbuffet* gave us an opportunity to laugh at both "high culture" and the pretense of gastronomic and artistic connoisseurship. What was so liberating about the endeavor was its delicious silliness. We could indulge and delight in the most basic and important essence of creative activity: the sheer sensory pleasure that creation, and its appreciation, can bring.

The *Le Corbuffet* food events, and this book, are thus based on a very simple idea: that perhaps there is a way to reintegrate the presence of art in everyday life, or *arte-vita*, through cooking, experimentation, and play. Perhaps creativity does not require expensive equipment or rare ingredients. Perhaps there is a way to take what has been done before, and make it your own. Perhaps perfection should be regarded with suspicion. Perhaps there is something revolutionary in the idea that anyone can make anything, especially things meant for sharing, using ordinary things.

This cookbook situates itself within a legacy of artworks that adopted the format of the cookbook to explore how rituals can provide a space for play and invention—to question how and why it is that we do the things we do. Consider *The Futurist Cookbook* (1932), in which F. T. Marinetti rallied for the political possibilities of a low-carb diet. Or, Salvador Dalí's opulently illustrated ode to gastronomic surrealism, *Les Dîners de Gala* (1972), which featured an array of sensual delicacies in unusual formats and situations.

Yet, importantly, it also hopes to suggest that hospitality—the art of sharing—can be a platform for critical and political practice. These days, when privatized and unequal access to the commons has become the norm, there is nothing simple nor straightforward about preparing a meal for one another. The kitchen and the dinner table can thus become imaginative contact zones for asking questions about how we wish to live, together, and what conventions, or constructions, prevent us from doing so.

Le Corbuffet attempts to play with humor as a form of resistance, by twisting idioms in art, food, and design, and playing with perceptions. Some of the recipes gambol with puns, while others try to imagine equivalences between ingredients, materials, and processes. Like event scores, the recipes prompt an engagement with techniques, concepts, and formats—from the kitchen, to the studio, and back again—to explore how ingredients can be transformed, assembled, and shaped. I invite you to enact the event score, and improvise—or rewrite it—at will, remixing mediums for maximum sensory, spatial, and social stimulation. Each recipe, like a story, artwork, dish, or building, starts with an idea, often borrowed and reimagined, to have its meaning and spirit renewed. My attempt in these recipes is to nod to the original dishes and art forms in their respective formats, while allowing creative alchemy to take flight.

I will admit that the recipes in *Le Corbuffet* brought me perverse amounts of pleasure to concoct and devise. It became a mild obsession to imagine how a deconstructed chocolate mud cake could embody the heady earthiness of Walter De Maria's *Earth Room* (1977) in taste, texture, and smell, or how a whipped cloud of matcha cream could offset a milky flan-as-filament in the manner of Dan Flavin's fluorescent sculptures. How might a green goddess dressing of a kale salad take cues from the intrepid boldness of Frida Kahlo? Or, could the silky flesh of corn purée, when pierced by crimson, bloodshot hot pepper, encapsulate the punctum required for a Chris Burden Shooter? These are some of the questions that kept me up at night.

Despite its absurdity, I gave myself full permission to follow my curiosity into strange territory after following numerous prods from the universe. After all, the impulse to create is a fundamental part of being human, and every act of creativity is an exercise in transformation. This book aspires to give you and your guests license to celebrate the unlimited pleasure that making, learning, and sharing bring—in the kitchen, the studio, and beyond.

Mies van der Roe Dip

Mies van der Roe Dip

Makes 1½ to 2 cups (375 to 500 g)

Inspired by the modernist German architect who abided by the maxim, "God is in the details," this mustard caviar is a satisfying congeal of pearlescent crunch. Though minuscule, its mustard seeds' hard exteriors swell and soften in a honey and vinegar mixture, transforming them into little eggs that burst with flavor and complexity. Consider this the next time you want a "less is more" approach for your plate-glass crudités platter or pretzel tower.

¼	cup	(33 g)	yellow mustard seeds
¼	cup	(33 g)	brown mustard seeds
¼	cup	(85 g)	honey
½	cup	(120 ml)	rice vinegar
¼	cup	(60 ml)	white wine vinegar or apple cider vinegar
½	tbsp		kosher salt

Steps

1   In a saucepan, bring mustard seeds, honey, both vinegars, salt, and ¾ cup (180 ml) water to a low, rolling boil over medium-low heat.

2   Reduce the heat to a simmer and cook, stirring often, until the mustard seeds swell and become tender but are still semi-firm, 40 minutes. During this time, the vinegar and honey will begin to smell malty and caramel-like. Add additional tablespoons of water if the mixture appears dry.

3   Remove the saucepan from the heat and let the mixture cool to room temperature.

4   Transfer the mustard caviar to an airtight container. Store in the refrigerator for up to 2 weeks.

Mies van der Roe Dip

Diller Scofidio + Renfro
Pickles

Diller Scofidio + Renfro Pickles

Makes 12 pint (0.5 l) jars

Compared with other forms of preservation, pickling is as much a process of looking as it is waiting. In this dill pickle recipe, which can be adapted to suit other vegetables,* Kirby cucumbers are subject to an interrogation of vision under glass as they marinate in an acidic network of brine, spices, and herbs. After a four-week period of anaerobic fermentation, they emerge, triumphant, having achieved the delectable and crunchy status of voyeuristic immortality.

5–6 pounds (2.3–2.7 kg)	**firm Kirby cucumbers,** chilled
3 tbsp	kosher salt
4 cups (960 ml)	white vinegar
	In each jar:
2–3 cloves	garlic, split
1 sprig	fresh dill
½ tsp	black peppercorns
½ tsp	coriander seeds
¼ tsp	celery seeds
–	Sterilized pint jars
–	Lids
–	Jar rings

Steps

1   Prepare the jars: Place the garlic cloves, dill, peppercorns, and seeds in sterilized pint jars. Tightly pack the cucumbers into the jars, leaving approximately a ½ inch (1.25 cm) of space near the mouth of each jar.

2   Make the brine: In a pot, bring the kosher salt, vinegar, and 2 cups (480 ml) water to a boil, stirring until the salt is dissolved. Reduce the heat to low and keep warm. Remove the saucepan from the heat and let the mixture cool to room temperature.

3   Assemble the jars: Pour the brine into the jars, leaving a ¼ inch (7 mm) of space at the mouth of each jar. Place the lids and jar rings on the jars and tighten. Let cool to room temperature.

4   Store the pickles in the refrigerator or proceed with the canning process. While the pickles can be eaten within 10 days, they are best consumed after 4 weeks.

*   Try subjecting other vegetables to this briny surveillance. Cauliflower, green beans, okra, tomatillos, carrots, onions, beets, and unripe tomatoes are all excellent substitutes. You are encouraged to add ½ teaspoon fennel seeds and ½ teaspoon mustard seeds, along with any other herbs or spices you fancy. When selecting produce, avoid soft and starchy vegetables. Instead, look for vegetables that have a high-water content and tight cellular structure. Quickly blanching the vegetables before canning will allow them to stay firmer and retain their color.

Diller Scofidio + Renfro Pickles

Florence Knoll Rolls

Florence Knoll Rolls

Makes 24 dinner rolls

Only timeless dinner rolls would do for the legendary American architect and furniture designer Florence Knoll. Unfussy and unadorned, these buttery pillows infused with herbs require no excess decoration. Based on modernist ideals, their clean lines and straightforward simplicity highlight the sensation of their light texture. As an essential functional element in your dinner composition, Florence Knoll Rolls can be transformed into virtually any dimension to add structure, organization, and direction to the "total design" of a culinary experience.

⅔	cup	(150 g)	sour cream or plain Greek yogurt
½	cup	(120 ml)	milk, preferably 2% or whole
1	large		egg, beaten
3	tbsp	(45 g)	unsalted butter, melted; plus more for greasing and glazing after baking
3	cups	(360 g)	unbleached all-purpose flour
3	tbsp		granulated sugar
2	tsp		instant yeast
1	tsp		kosher salt

| 4 | tbsp | finely chopped fresh herbs, such as thyme or chives |

Steps

1. Using an electric mixer, or by hand, mix all of the ingredients in a large bowl. Knead the mixture until a smooth, soft, and sticky alabaster dough forms, 5 to 10 minutes. Transfer the dough to a greased bowl and cover. Let the dough rise until swollen in size, though not quite doubled, 60 to 90 minutes.

2. Butter a 9 x 13-inch (23 x 33 cm) baking dish. Portion the dough into 24 balls. Transfer the rolls to the prepared pan. Cover and let the rolls puff again, until they are touching, about 60 minutes.

3. Preheat the oven to 350°F (180°C). Bake the rolls until they turn golden brown, 20 to 25 minutes. Once out of the oven, brush the tops with melted butter for added flavor. Transfer to a wire rack to let cool. Store baked rolls in an airtight container at room temperature for several days, or freeze.

Chris Burden Shooters

Chris Burden Shooters

Makes 10 shooters

Like *Shoot* (1971), Chris Burden's controversial performance, in which the artist deliberately received a bullet to his arm, this dish delivers a quick blast of heat and smoky paprika to unsuspecting palates. A silken corn purée becomes the perfect carrier for this experience of self-inflicted shock.

6	ears	corn, shucked
5	cups (1.2 l)	low-sodium vegetable broth
1	cup (240 ml)	milk, preferably 2% or reduced-fat
2	tbsp (30 g)	unsalted butter
1	small	onion, preferably Vidalia, diced (about 1 cup/142 g)
1	sprig	fresh thyme
1		bay leaf
to	taste	kosher salt and black pepper
—		Tabasco or favorite hot sauce

— Smoked paprika

— Nutritional yeast (optional)

Steps

1. Cut kernels from cobs and set aside. In a pot, bring the corn cobs, vegetable broth, and milk to a boil. Reduce heat to medium-low and simmer for 15 to 20 minutes. Using tongs, remove the cobs from the broth. Discard the cobs and let the broth cool.

2. In a second large pot, melt the butter over medium heat. Add diced onions, thyme, and bay leaf and sauté until the onions turn glossy, 10 minutes. (Do not allow the onions to brown.) Add the corn kernels to the pot and sauté the vegetables for a few minutes. Season with salt and pepper.

3. Add the warm broth to the onions and corn. Simmer over medium-low heat for 20 minutes. Discard the bay leaf and thyme.

4. Transfer the corn soup to a blender and purée until smooth, being careful when blending hot liquids. Season with salt and pepper, if desired. Strain the mixture through a sieve. Let the soup cool, then chill in the refrigerator for a minimum of 2 hours or overnight.

5. To serve, ladle a few spoonfuls of corn soup into shot glasses. Add a dash of Tabasco sauce and a sprinkle of paprika. For extra richness, sprinkle nutritional yeast over the corn soup before adding the Tabasco and paprika.

Chris Burden Shooters

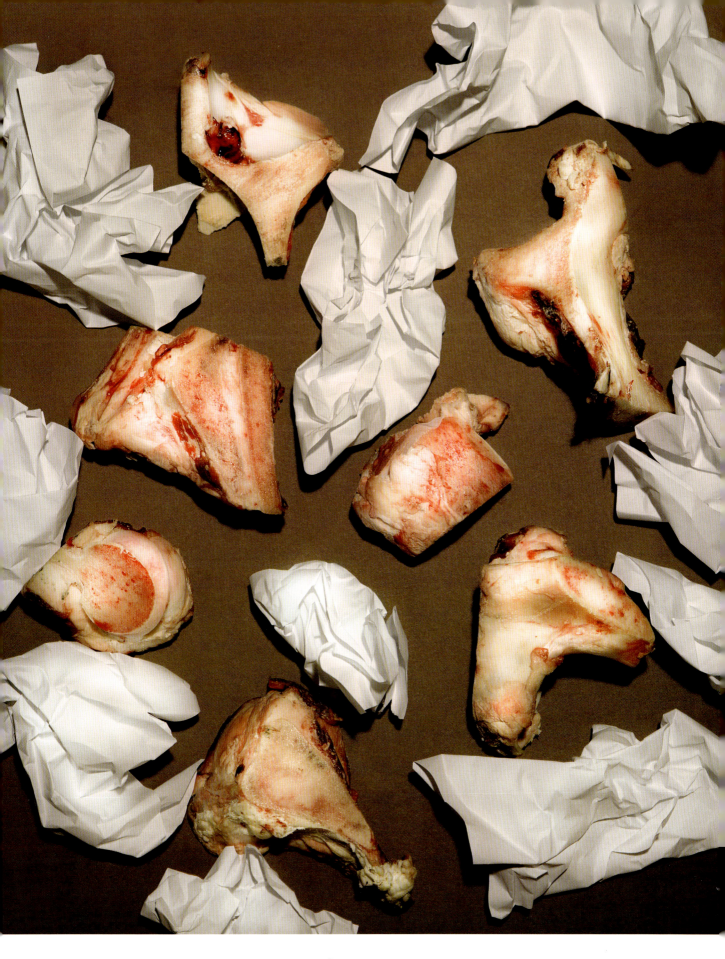

Raymond Pettibone Broth

Raymond Pettibone Broth

Makes 1 gallon (3.7 l)

Pen and paper, bones and water. Sometimes that's all you need. Like
drawing, boiling bones has been an elemental part of the creative process for
centuries. Don't let the sheen of its current popularity and commercialism
fool you. Making bone broth is humble, instinctive, and unpretentious.
It requires virtually no expertise, rendering it the ultimate antiauthoritarian
form of cooking. Stripped down to its rudiments, the basis for the most
seemingly complicated dishes, irrespective of genre, script, or narrative,
is broken down and starkly exposed. You can add additional flavoring
agents for color or spice, but sticking to the basics communicates a profound
message that is refreshingly clear. When pared down, an empowering truth
to cooking is revealed: that anyone, really, can do it.

2	pounds	beef bones
(908 g)		

2	tsp	apple cider vinegar

		Flavoring agents (optional)
1		onion
2		carrots
2		celery stalks
1	tbsp	sea salt
1	tsp	black peppercorns

Steps

1   In a 5-quart (4.7 l) stockpot, combine the beef bones with enough cold water to cover the bones. Add the vinegar and let the bones sit in the water for 30 minutes to 1 hour. Discard the water. Rinse the bones and return them to the pot.

2   Fill the pot with enough fresh water to cover and place it on a burner over high heat. Add the flavoring agents (if using) and bring to a vigorous boil. Reduce the heat to low and simmer, partially covered, for 8 hours or more. Make sure that the liquid does not become too hot and boil over.

3   In the first few hours, the surface of the broth will yield foamy impurities; skim and discard. Occasionally add more water to the pot if the level of broth decreases considerably. You will notice that as the bone marrow and cartilage break down with time, the broth will become thick and opaque. This is good.

4   After the desired levels of flavor and richness are achieved, remove the pot from the heat. Cool and strain the liquid to remove the bones and flavoring agents. Store the broth in an airtight container in the refrigerator for up to 1 week, or freeze. Once chilled, the broth will appear gelatinous—an excellent achievement.

Raymond Pettibone Broth

John   McCrackers

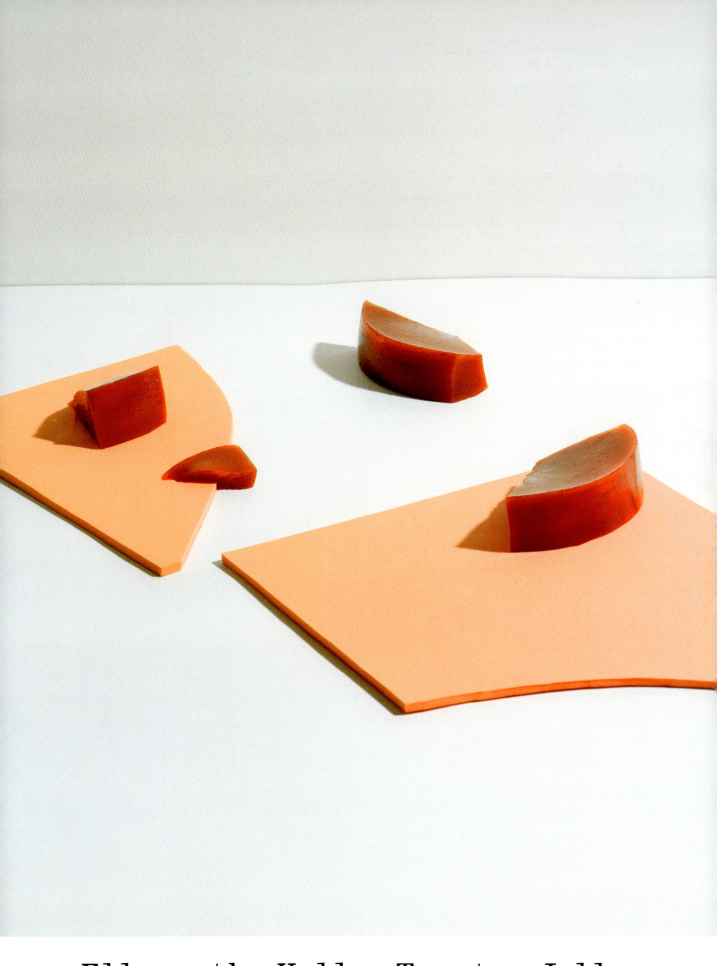

Ellsworth Kelly Tomato Jelly

Ellsworth Kelly Tomato Jelly

Serves 8 to 10

An unconventional and wobbly study of form, color, and shape, this brilliant tomato aspic takes its cue from Ellsworth Kelly's irregularly shaped canvases. To serve and eat this jelly is to engage in a courageous bodily encounter of bold, tomato abstraction—at once asserting its own space and autonomy, while being responsive to the sensations and gestures of its eater.

2	tbsp	unflavored gelatin
4	cups (960 ml)	tomato juice
2	tbsp	finely minced onion
3	tsp	granulated sugar
1	tsp	kosher salt
1	tsp	tamari or Worcestershire sauce
¼	tsp	celery seeds
2		bay leaves
2	whole	cloves
2	tbsp	fresh lemon juice

Steps

1. Prepare the gelatin: In a small bowl, combine the gelatin with ¼ cup (60 ml) cold water. Let it sit for a few minutes. Add ¼ cup (60 ml) hot water and whisk to dissolve the gelatin. Set aside.

2. Prepare the spiced tomato filling: In a large saucepan, combine the tomato juice, onion, sugar, salt, tamari, celery seeds, bay leaves, and cloves. Bring the mixture to a boil. Reduce the heat to low and simmer, stirring occasionally, for 10 to 15 minutes. Over a large bowl, strain the tomato mixture through a sieve.

3. Make the aspic: Add the gelatin and lemon juice and stir until well combined. Spray a ring mold or 7-inch (18 cm) soufflé dish, liberally, with a neutral-flavored oil. Carefully pour the mixture into the prepared dish. Chill, covered, in the refrigerator until set, about 6 hours.

Martin Parrfait

Jorge Pardo Whipped Lardo

Jorge Pardo Whipped Lardo

Makes 1 pint jar (0.5 l)

For Cuban-American sculptor Jorge Pardo, a lamp is not merely a lamp, and a tile is not merely a tile; they are opportunities to explore the intersections of sculpture, architecture, and design, and defy expectations. Likewise, this whipped spread takes an ingredient typically thought of as grease, often used to flavor other dishes, and transforms it into a substantive culinary indulgence. Add air and motion, and a block of cured fat becomes a creamy, delectable delight. Infused with garlic and rosemary, these whipped fluffy clouds of porky cream taste like the best butter you've ever had.

½	pound (227 g)	lardo (or cured bacon like guanciale)
1	head	garlic, roasted and skins removed
1	tbsp	fresh rosemary
½	tsp	kosher salt
¼	tsp	black pepper

Steps

1 Finely dice the lardo (or guanciale), or, better yet, grind it using a ⅛-inch (3 mm) die.

2 In a food processor, combine all ingredients. Whip continuously at high speed for 10 to 15 minutes. You may need to take a few breaks if your contraption gets too hot. The mixture should aerate and eventually become very light and fluffy.

3 Serve immediately with crostini or store the lardo in an airtight container in the refrigerator for up to 1 week.

Alvar and Aino Avocaalto Bowl

Frei Otto Frittata

Frei Otto Frittata

Serves 6

German architect Frei Otto was obsessed with soap bubbles and weightlessness. Like his name, meaning "free" in German, he was driven by a desire to liberate structures from gravitational forces, such that they could seem lighter than air. Tensile systems and membranes became the means by which he stretched unconventional materials, allowing new, elastic configurations to take shape, almost organically. This breakfast adopts Otto's interest in the substantive and the ethereal. Air is treated as a structural material, allowing the volume of egg whites to inflate exponentially into a heavenly balloon. Soaring above a savory base of beet greens and potatoes, the soufflé holds its shape for roughly half an hour after being baked, transforming the egg creation into a brief performance. The result is a frittata reimagined: airy, lightweight, and thrillingly impermanent.

2	tbsp	olive oil
2	medium	potatoes, diced
2	bunches	beet greens, sliced
1	clove	garlic, minced
1	cup (240 ml)	whole milk
3	tbsp (45 g)	unsalted butter, plus more for greasing
3	tbsp	unbleached all-purpose flour

¼	tsp	cayenne pepper
pinch		nutmeg
4		egg yolks, at room temperature
5		egg whites, at room temperature
¼	tsp	cream of tartar
1	cup (113 g)	Gruyère or Emmental cheese, grated
¼	cup (28 g)	Parmesan cheese, grated, plus more for dusting
2	tbsp	chives or other herbs

Steps

1   Preheat the oven to 400°F (200°C).

2   Cook the vegetables: In a large skillet, heat the olive oil over medium heat. Add the diced potatoes and sauté until fork-tender. Add the beet greens and garlic and continue to cook until the greens wilt, several minutes longer.

3   Make the béchamel: In a small saucepan, gently heat the milk over medium-low heat. Set aside and keep warm. In another medium saucepan, melt the butter over medium-low heat. Whisk the flour into the melted butter. Cook the mixture, stirring constantly, for a few minutes. Slowly pour the warm milk into the flour, whisking constantly to avoid lumps, and cook until the béchamel thickens. Remove the béchamel from the heat.

4   Stir the cayenne pepper and nutmeg into the béchamel sauce. Slowly whisk in the egg yolks.

5   Whip the egg whites: In the bowl of a stand mixer fitted with the whisk attachment, beat the egg whites and cream of tartar until stiff peaks form.

6   Fold the egg whites into the egg-béchamel mixture, being careful not to deflate the air that you created. Gently fold the Gruyère, Parmesan, and chives into the eggs.

7   Assemble the frittata: Butter a soufflé dish and dust with Parmesan cheese. Evenly distribute the potatoes and greens at the bottom of the prepared dish.

8   Carefully pour the soufflé mixture into the dish. With your thumb, rub the inner rim of the dish so it is clean of any soufflé. Bake until the top is golden, 30 minutes. Serve immediately.

Frei Otto Frittata

Amazing Plug-in Archigramola

Amazing Plug-in Archigramola

Makes 7 cups (854 g)

Just as the British architectural collective Archigram imagined flexible megastructures that would power the city of the future, granola represents the ultimate infrastructural energy snack. Its insoluble fibers are excellent for maintaining the human megamachine's digestive networks. Like modular building materials, granola clusters can be formed or molded into slabs and bars. An excellent carrier of flavors, this base recipe can be "plugged-in" with different combinations of ingredients, both savory and sweet. (See note at end of recipe.) This is megafood at its finest, offering an instant zap of nutrient-rich energy when you need to zoom.

3	cups	(297 g)	rolled oats
1	cup	(140 g)	raw, unsalted pumpkin seeds (pepitas)
1	cup	(140 g)	raw, unsalted sunflower seeds
1	cup	(60 g)	unsweetened coconut flakes
1¼	cups	(86 g)	sliced almonds, roughly chopped
¾	cup	(180 ml)	good-quality maple syrup
¼	cup	(60 ml)	extra-virgin olive oil
2	tbsp		golden syrup (optional)

Steps

1.   Preheat the oven to 300°F (150°C). Line 1 or 2 rimmed baking sheets with parchment paper.

2.   In a large bowl, combine all the ingredients.

3.   Carefully spread the granola mixture in an even layer on the lined baking sheet. (If granola doesn't fit on 1 sheet, you may need to divide it between 2 rimmed baking sheets.)

4.   Bake, stirring every 20 minutes, until the oats are toasted, 45 minutes to 1 hour.

5.   Store granola in an airtight container. To preserve its freshness, store it in the freezer.

Plug-Ins: The granola can be customized by adding flavorings like cinnamon, vanilla, nutmeg, brown sugar, or honey before baking. Dried fruit can be added after the granola has cooled. For a savory version, dust the granola with Aleppo pepper and za'atar (omit the coconut flakes) before baking. Enjoy with a savory yogurt flavored with garlic, lemon, and sea salt.

Quiche Haring

Quiche Haring

Serves 6 to 8

Growing up in the quiet Pennsylvania Dutch borough of Kutztown, Pennsylvania, ten-year-old Keith Haring dreamt of being an artist in France. Later, as an art student, he moved to New York City in the late 1970s, magnetized by its bustling graffiti and thriving alternative art scene. Drawing elaborate murals in subway stations and street corners, atop billboards and signs, he was dedicated to promoting art as an accessible experience that should be shared. This quiche, inspired by Haring's dream of becoming an artist in France, is an homage to his small-town roots and big-city career. The buttery, yeasted dough of a Pennsylvania Dutch onion pie (or *zwiebelkuchen*) takes its cues from the iconic New York "everything" bagel. Flecked with poppy seeds, sesame, caraway, and onion, this quiche is a treat reminiscent of a bacon-and-egg bagel sandwich that is meant to be enjoyed in public space—on the street, in the subway, on the bus—with others, as a celebration of the city.

For the dough

2	tsp	instant yeast
¾	cup (180 ml)	2% or whole milk, warmed
3¼	cups (390 g)	unbleached all-purpose flour, plus more for dusting
2	large	eggs
½	cup	unsalted butter, at room
	(1 stick/115 g)	temperature, plus more for greasing
1¼	tsp	kosher salt
1	tsp	sesame seeds
1	tsp	poppy seeds
1	tsp	onion flakes

For the filling

3	strips	thickly cut bacon,	diced
2	medium	onions,	finely chopped
4	large	eggs	
1	cup (227 g)	crème fraîche	
½	tsp	kosher salt	
½	tsp	black pepper	
¼	tsp	caraway seeds	

Steps

1   Make the dough: In a small bowl, dissolve the yeast in the warm milk.

2   In the bowl of a stand mixer fitted with the dough hook, combine the flour, eggs, yeasted milk, butter, and salt. Knead the mixture on medium speed. The dough will be a pale yellow and seem slightly wet. Distribute the sesame seeds, poppy seeds, and onion flakes into the dough and continue to knead, occasionally scraping the sides of the bowl, until a soft ball forms.

3   Place the dough in a lightly greased bowl. Cover the bowl and let the dough rise until puffy, about 1 hour. After this period, you can continue to let the dough rise slowly in the refrigerator for up to 24 hours, which will intensify its flavor.

4   Make the filling: In a skillet, brown the bacon until crisp. Carefully transfer the bacon bits to a paper towel–lined plate to absorb the grease. Let the bacon cool to room temperature.

5   In the remaining bacon grease, sauté the chopped onions over medium-low heat until caramelized and golden brown. Let the onions cool to room temperature.

6   In a large bowl, beat the eggs. Stir in the crème fraîche, salt, pepper, and caraway seeds until well combined.

Quiche Haring

7   Prepare the pastry: Lightly butter a 9-inch (23 cm) springform cake pan. Transfer the rested dough onto a lightly floured work surface. Roll out the dough into an approximately 15-inch (38 cm) circle.

8   Transfer the dough to the prepared cake pan, using your hands to press the dough into the sides. Make sure the dough runs the height of the cake pan's sides, exceeding it so there's a slight lip on the rim of the pan. Let the dough rise and puff again for 45 minutes.

9   Assemble the quiche: Preheat the oven to 350°F (180°C). Scatter the pieces of bacon and caramelized onions evenly on the bottom of the proofed pastry. Pour in the egg-caraway filling. Bake until the dough is lightly golden brown and the filling is set, 50 to 60 minutes. Let it cool slightly before cutting and serving.

Lella and Massimo Vignelli
Pignoli Cookies

R. Crumb Satirical Topping

R. Crumb Satirical Topping

Serves 2 to 4

Crumb toppings are a staple of many American fruit-based treats, but we all know that the fruit is simply a foil for the delectable topping. Inspired by Robert Crumb's exaggerated iconography of American culture, this satirical topping shuns any seasonal ingredients in favor of a singular, delightfully scatological mound of buttery morsel. For a cheap thrill, munch on this lowbrow breakfast with a hot mug of boozy coffee or tea, forgetting the cutlery altogether. It'll be our dirty little secret.

1½ cups	(180 g)	unbleached all-purpose flour
1 cup	(100 g)	rolled oats
1 cup (2 sticks/225 g)		unsalted butter, cubed and cold
¾ cup	(150 g)	granulated sugar
¾ cup	(150 g)	light or dark brown sugar
½ tsp		kosher salt
½ tsp		ground cinnamon

Steps

1   Preheat the oven to 350°F (180°C). Line a baking sheet with parchment paper.

2   In the bowl of a stand mixer fitted with the paddle attachment and set to low speed, combine all the ingredients. (Don't skimp on the butter; gratuitousness is pleasure.) Alternatively, you can use your hands, rubbing the butter and flour quickly to ensure the butter remains cold. Mix until the butter is roughly the size of large chunks of gravel and the crumbly mixture holds together.

3   Scoop the mixture onto the center of the lined baking sheet. Mold it gently into an exaggerated mound that is both slightly neurotic and gratifyingly voluptuous.

4   Bake until golden brown, 35 to 40 minutes. Enjoy while warm.

R. Crumb Satirical Topping

William Eggleston Strata

William Eggleston Strata

Serves 8 to 10

A purveyor of all things American, William Eggleston, the great legend of color photography, was a lover of casseroles. He developed a casserole recipe of his own, consisting, largely, of processed cheese, grits, and butter. While this strata adopts slightly loftier culinary ambitions, it sticks to the classic casserole formula of bread, eggs, milk, and cheese. Known as the "poor man's pudding," this no-nonsense breakfast is friendly to whatever resources your refrigerator, and coin purse, may hold.

5	cups	(455 g)	cubed stale bread
2½	cups	(600 ml)	milk, preferably whole
8			eggs
1	cup	(227 g)	plain Greek yogurt
¼	tsp		cayenne pepper
½	tsp		kosher or sea salt
¼	tsp		black pepper
¼	tsp		paprika
pinch			nutmeg
3			scallions, chopped

1 cup	cooked vegetables such as
(about 156 g)	sautéed mushrooms or steamed broccoli (optional)

1½ cups (184 g)	cheddar cheese, grated

Steps

1   Prepare the bread cubes: Cut stale bread into 2-inch (5 cm) cubes. (If using fresh or day-old bread, toast slices on a baking sheet in the oven for a few minutes to dry it out.) Set aside.

2   Prepare the egg custard: In a medium bowl, beat the milk, eggs, and Greek yogurt. Add the cayenne, salt, pepper, paprika, and nutmeg to the egg mixture and mix well.

3   Layer the strata: Butter a 9 x 13-inch (23 x 33 cm) casserole or baking dish with 2-inch (5 cm) sides and place the bread cubes in the buttered dish. Scatter the scallions, any additional vegetables (if using), and half the cheddar cheese over the bread, distributing them evenly.

4   Pour the egg custard over the bread, ensuring that all of the bread makes contact with the mixture. Sprinkle the remaining cheese over the soggy bread. Cover and chill in the refrigerator for 2 hours, or overnight.

5   Bake the strata: Remove the strata from the refrigerator and allow it to come to room temperature. Preheat the oven to 375°F (190°C). Bake the strata until golden brown, 30 minutes. Broil on low heat for an additional few minutes to brown the cheese. Serve immediately.

Bananni   Albers   Babka

Bananni Albers Babka

Makes 1 loaf

Twisted strands of vanilla, halva, and chocolate braid this banana loaf inspired by the Jewish-German textile artist and printmaker Anni Albers, who revolutionized fiber arts with her distinctive graphic sensibility and technical ingenuity. As head of the weaving workshop at the Bauhaus in the early 1930s, Albers regarded the studio as a laboratory, pushing the old craft of the loom into new territory. You, too, are encouraged to innovate with this unconventional take on a traditional recipe. Experiment with different fillings in the babka: add nuts, dried fruit, or keep it plain—for iteration, like variety, is the spice of creative life.

For the yeasted dough

2	tsp		dry yeast
5	tbsp		2% or whole milk, warmed
3½	cups	(420 g)	unbleached all-purpose flour, plus more for dusting
3	tbsp		granulated sugar
6	tbsp	(90 g)	unsalted butter, at room temperature, plus more for greasing
1	large		egg
3			bananas, mashed

For the vanilla halva spread

1	cup	(150 g)	tahini
1	tsp		pure vanilla extract
1	tsp		ground cinnamon

2	tsp		fresh lemon juice

For the chocolate spread

3	tbsp	(45 g)	unsalted butter
½	cup	(85 g)	semisweet chocolate chips
1	tbsp		Dutch-processed cocoa powder

Steps

1   Make the yeasted dough: Dissolve the yeast in the warm milk for a few minutes, allowing it to bloom.

2   In the bowl of a stand mixer set to low speed and fitted with the dough hook, combine the flour, sugar, and salt. With the motor running, add the yeast. Add the butter and egg and continue to mix. Slowly incorporate the mashed bananas. Mix at medium speed until the dough becomes a ball, about 5 minutes. Chill the dough, covered, in the refrigerator for 6 hours (or overnight).

3   Make the vanilla halva spread: In a bowl, combine the tahini, vanilla, cinnamon, and lemon juice, stirring until smooth.

4   Make the chocolate spread: In a small saucepan, melt the butter over medium-low heat. Add the chocolate chips and the cocoa, whisking until smooth. Set aside to let cool to room temperature.

5   Time to weave: Generously butter a loaf pan. Line the base with parchment paper, leaving an overhang on both sides to facilitate lifting the loaf once baked.

6   Tip the proofed yeasted dough onto a lightly floured surface. Roll out the dough into a rectangle about 12 x 16 inches (30 x 40 cm), and ⅛-inch (3 mm) thick. If the dough begins to soften too much, chill it on a tray in the refrigerator for 10 minutes.

7   With the shorter edge of the rectangle nearest you, spread the halva filling over the left half of the dough and the chocolate filling over the right half, or vice versa, making sure the filling reaches the corners of the dough. Roll the dough tightly from left to right, like a jelly roll, to create a coiled log. Using a sharp knife or pastry cutter, cut the dough in half along its length to produce 2 thin strips. You should be able to see both fillings in the form of layers.

8   Now, braid: Lay one piece over the other so they form an X.
     Then, working from their point of intersection, twist the strands over each other on both ends to form a plait.

9   Carefully place the braided dough into the prepared loaf pan.
     Tuck the ends under so the plait looks more or less symmetrical. Allow the dough to rise in a warm spot, until doubled in size, 1½ to 2 hours.

10   When the dough is almost ready, preheat the oven to 350°F (180°C).
     Bake the babka, rotating the pan halfway during the baking time, until the bread is beautifully browned and your kitchen is perfumed with its intoxicating aroma, about 50 minutes.

11   Let the babka cool in the pan. Crowds will begin to form quickly at this point. Store in an airtight container at room temperature.
     It also freezes well. But I doubt it will last that long.

Bananni Albers Babka

Darren Almond Cake

Darren Almond Cake

Makes one 9-inch (23 cm) cake

Darren Almond's photographs taken by the light of the moon depict ethereal landscapes, devoid of shadow and weight. This simple almond cake, in tribute to the artist's scenography, attempts to capture elements of the forest with its pine-scented cream and rosemary flecks of nutty crumb. Adorned with a light cloud of unsweetened whipped cream, it is best served at early sunrise while observing the stillness of the world unawake.

For the cake

2	cups (192 g)	almond flour
6	tbsp	unbleached all-purpose flour
1⅓	cups (267 g)	granulated sugar
¼–½	tsp	minced fresh rosemary
8		egg whites
½	tsp	kosher salt
1		lemon, zested

For the whipped cream

1½ cups (360 ml) heavy cream
2 tsp   pine syrup (optional)
sprigs   fresh Thai basil or
                  other herbs for garnish
                  (optional)

Steps

1 Preheat the oven to 350°F (180°C). Butter a 9-inch (23 cm) cake pan. Place a round of parchment paper on the bottom.

2 In a small bowl, combine the almond flour, all-purpose flour, sugar, and rosemary.

3 Using an electric mixer, beat the egg whites with the salt until they form stiff peaks. Slowly fold the dry mixture into the egg whites, adding a little at a time, until combined. Grate the zest of one lemon into the egg whites, and fold gently to incorporate.

4 Pour the batter into the prepared cake pan and bake until a toothpick inserted into the center of the cake comes out clean, 45 minutes to 1 hour. Let the cake cool on a wire rack before removing it from the pan.

5 To serve, whip the heavy cream until soft peaks form. Flavor the whipped cream with pine syrup, if using. Smooth it on top of the cake like icing, or serve on the side. Garnish with a sprinkling of fragrant edible herbs.

Darren Almond Cake

Rhubarbara   Kruger   Compote

Rhubarbara Kruger Compote

Makes 2 to 3 cups (650 to 975 g)

Like the crimson red that often punctuates Barbara Kruger's bold and unrelenting graphic iconography, this rhubarb and red currant compote translates the high contrast, acerbic punch of Kruger's installations into a lip-smacking sugar stew. Its ruby stain is further heightened by the addition of raspberry liqueur. Smear it over toast, on yogurt, atop a scoop of ice cream, or a billboard, on your arm, or even your kitchen counter. It adds power and punch to virtually any cultural construct, and at any scale.

1	pound	(454 g)	rhubarb stalks
1	cup	(140 g)	red currants
⅓	cup	(66 g)	granulated sugar
¼	cup	(60 ml)	Chambord, crème de cassis, or Crème Yvette

Steps

1   Cut the rhubarb into ½-inch (1.25 cm) pieces. Stem the currants.

2   In a saucepan, combine the rhubarb, currants, sugar, and liqueur. Cook over medium heat, stirring occasionally, until the mixture bubbles and the rhubarb and currants soften and release their juices, about 15 minutes. Let cool to room temperature.

3   Store in an airtight container in the refrigerator up to one week.

Anri *Dammi i Colori* Sala(d)

Anri *Dammi i Colori* Sala(d)

Serves 6 to 8

Like Anri Sala's 2003 film about the profound power of color in Tirana's urban transformation, this salad is the antidote to the drudgery of fiber and cellulose consumption. A spicy peanut dressing and fresh herbs transform a salad "that you are doomed to eat by fate" into a salad that "you choose to eat." Taking its cues from *karedok*, an Indonesian raw vegetable salad, virtually any contrasting selection of vegetables and fruit ranging in hue, shape, and crunch can be deployed. Experiment and go wild: leafy, watery, cruciferous, or sweet—the colorful combinations are endless when painted with this simple yet potent peanut dressing.

For the dressing

1	cup (270 g)	creamy peanut butter or almond butter
2	tsp	coconut sugar
1½	tbsp	tamari, coconut aminos, or soy sauce
3		limes, juiced
1	tbsp	coconut vinegar or rice vinegar
2½	tsp	fish sauce
1–2		fresh red chiles, seeded and chopped
2	cloves	garlic, grated or finely minced

For the vegetables

1	pound (454 g)	new potatoes, scrubbed
1	small	head of red cabbage
1	small	yellow squash
2–3		raw beets, peeled
1		orange carrot, trimmed and scrubbed
1		purple carrot, trimmed and scrubbed
15		cherry tomatoes
½		English cucumber
½	bunch	fresh cilantro
10		sugar snap peas, trimmed

–	Limes for garnish

Steps

1   Make the dressing: In a bowl, combine all the ingredients, adding ½ cup to ¾ cup (120 to 180 ml) water a spoonful at a time, stirring constantly, until the dressing loosens and the desired consistency is reached. Keep the dressing covered in an airtight container. The sauce tends to thicken as it sits, so you may need to thin with a few spoonfuls of water before adding it to your salad.

2   Prepare the vegetables: In a medium pot, parboil the potatoes until fork-tender. Drain, rinse well under cold water to stop the cooking process, and set aside.

3   Finely shred the cabbage. Using a mandoline or sharp knife, thinly slice the squash, beets, and carrots. Halve the cherry tomatoes and baby potatoes. Roughly chop the cucumber and the cilantro stems and leaves. Remove the strings from the sugar snap peas.

4   Paint the vegetables: In a large bowl, toss the potatoes, cabbage, squash, beets, carrots, cherry tomatoes, and cucumber with the dressing, making sure the dressing is distributed evenly. Gently fold in the cilantro, saving some for a garnish. Serve immediately with extra cilantro on top and additional wedges of lime.

Anri *Dammi i* Colori Sala(d)

Mario Botta Carota

Mario Botta Carota

Serves 4

For Mario Botta, architecture is not only about making objects. A site and the history of a place are the source from which a building, or culinary tradition, can grow and develop. In tribute to the Swiss architect, this recipe takes the humble roasted carrot, a fleshy enlarged taproot, as the ground from which an unusual combination of flavors is propagated. Inspired by Switzerland's invention of the carrot cake, a light, cardamom-infused yogurt balances the sweet flavors of a simple, blistered root—the origin of all great things.

2 bunches (about 488 g)	**young carrots,** trimmed and scrubbed
2–3 tbsp	olive oil
to taste	kosher salt and black pepper
1 cup (227 g)	plain Greek yogurt
1 tsp	ground cardamom
½ tsp	ground coriander
1 tsp	pomegranate molasses
squeeze	lemon
–	Fresh parsley or cilantro leaves

Steps

1   Preheat the oven to 400°F (200°C).

2   On a large rimmed baking sheet, combine the carrots and olive oil with a light dusting of salt and pepper. Roast the carrots until lightly browned, roughly 25 minutes.

3   In a medium bowl, mix the yogurt, cardamom, coriander, and pomegranate molasses. Add a squeeze of lemon. Season with salt and pepper. Garnish with a flurry of parsley or cilantro leaves.

4   Serve the roasted carrots stacked, with dollops of cardamom yogurt.

Mario Botta Carota

Kimchi Gordon

Kimchi Gordon

Makes about 8 pounds (3.6 kg) of kimchi

Irreverent, unconventional, and an icon of spiciness, Kim Gordon has created her own iconographic ecosystem. From music and paintings to sculpture and installations, her approach to each art form can be characterized by a sophisticated messiness and improvisational spirit. Likewise, kimchi is a dish that stands proud in its singularity, a kind of scorching, rapscallion critique on the simple sourness of most fermented foods. Wild and untamed, it defies categorization. Neither condiment nor accompaniment, it is always uncompromising and plays side dish to no one.

For salting the cabbage

6 pounds (2.7 kg)	Napa cabbage or Chinese cabbage (roughly 2 large heads)
½ cup (125 g)	kosher salt

For the rice paste

2 tbsp	sweet rice flour
¼ cup (50 g)	sugar, preferably turbinado

For the spices and aromatics

3–4	dried anchovies
24 cloves	garlic, roughly chopped (roughly 1½ heads of garlic)

1	2-inch	(5 cm)	piece of ginger, roughly chopped
1			white onion, minced
½	cup	(120 ml)	fish sauce
2	cups	(200 g)	Korean red chile flakes (*gochugaru*)

For the vegetables

2	cups	(220 g)	julienned Korean radish (*mu*) or daikon radish
2	cups	(220 g)	julienned carrots
8			scallions, chopped
1	cup	(56 g)	fresh chives, preferably Asian chives (*buchu*)

–	Food-safe rubber gloves

–	Sanitized glass jars or stainless-steel food storage containers

Steps

1   First, tenderize the cabbage: Begin by quartering each head of cabbage lengthwise, so the leaves are still held together at their base. Carefully remove the tough core at the heart of each stem, such that the leaves are still intact. Wash the cabbage well, removing any damaged outer leaves.

2   In the largest bowl imaginable, evenly sprinkle the cabbage quarters with kosher salt. Place a large plate or pot atop the cabbage pieces with some additional weights added (*S,M,L,XL* or *Janson's History of Art* work beautifully). Let the cabbage tenderize for a minimum of 2 hours.

Make sure to rotate the cabbage pieces to drain any liquid that is released periodically.

3 Once the cellulose is tender and pliable, wash the cabbage pieces thoroughly, making sure to run water between the cabbage leaves, to remove the salt. (The cabbage at this stage should taste mildly salty but not overwhelmingly so.)

4 While the cabbage tenderizes, make the rice paste: In a small pot, combine the sweet rice flour and sugar with 2 cups (480 ml) water. Whisk over medium heat until the mixture comes to a boil. Reduce heat to low and simmer, whisking periodically, until the mixture thickens to a porridge-like consistency. Remove from heat and let cool to room temperature.

5 Blend the spices and aromatics: In a food processor, blitz the dried anchovies until they form a paste. Add the garlic, ginger, and onion, and purée until smooth.

6 Add the cooled rice paste, fish sauce, and chile flakes to this mixture. Transfer this aromatic spice paste to a large bowl and combine with the julienned vegetables, scallions, and chives.

7 Armed with rubber gloves, take each cabbage quarter and smear the vegetable-spice paste mixture between the cabbage leaves liberally, making sure that the outer leaves are also coated.

8 Place each cabbage quarter in sanitized stainless-steel kimchi containers or large glass jars, packing each jar tightly. If you can't find large kimchi containers, you can also chop the cabbage leaves into 2 x 1-inch (5 x 2.5 cm) pieces, making sure to compress the spiced cabbage firmly into the vessel. Take any remaining paste and distribute it over and around the cabbage pieces in the container.

9 Begin the fermentation process: Seal the containers with tight-fitting lids. Store at room temperature, away from direct light, for 2 to 3 days.

10 Gently shake the jars to distribute the liquid that is released by the cabbage. By the third day, this liquid should fizz and bubble. Transfer the containers to the refrigerator.

11 Shake the jars daily to distribute this liquid. Allow the kimchi to ferment for 14 to 18 days. The kimchi should be consumed within 30 to 45 days of reaching peak fermentation.

Kimchi Gordon

Frida Kale-o Salad

Frida Kale-o Salad

Serves 8

Like Frida Kahlo's piercing gaze, the natural world, depicted in the artist's landscapes, is arresting, sovereign, and confident of its own worth. Both healer and instigator, it is abundant and all-knowing, yet it also contains secrets, which, with a sly smile, we know it will never make known. If the work of a salad is to translate the sensations of the natural world to your plate, this dish is an attempt to offer an experience that is nothing short of the overwhelming complexity and contradiction that has come to characterize the verdant terrain of Kahlo's cosmos—mysterious, elusive, and soulful.

For the green goddess dressing

1		poblano pepper
–		olive oil, for brushing
1		avocado, pitted
2½	cups (600 ml)	buttermilk
1	clove	garlic
2		limes, juiced
1	tsp	capers, rinsed and drained
1		jalapeño, seeded
⅓	cup (15 g)	fresh cilantro leaves
¼	tsp	ground cumin
½	tsp	sea salt
¼	tsp	black pepper

For the breaded tomatillos

8			tomatillos, husks removed
½	cup	(60 g)	unbleached all-purpose flour
¼	tsp		sea salt, plus more for sprinkling
⅛	tsp		black pepper
1			egg, beaten
½	cup	(25 g)	panko bread crumbs
1	tbsp	(15 g)	unsalted butter
1	tbsp		olive oil

For the salad

2	bunches	kale, ribs removed, shredded
1–2		ripe avocados, sliced or scooped

Steps

1   Roast the poblano pepper: If using an oven, preheat the oven to 425°F (220°C). Brush the poblano with olive oil. Roast it on a baking sheet, turning halfway through, until the skin chars, 30 to 40 minutes. If using a gas stove, roast the poblano on the grate of a burner. Use tongs to turn it periodically, until the skin chars. Transfer the roasted poblano to a bowl, cover, and let it steam for 15 minutes. Pull the skins off. Seed and set aside.

2   Make the dressing: In a blender, combine the roasted poblano, avocado flesh, buttermilk, garlic, lime juice, capers, jalapeño, cilantro, cumin, salt, and pepper. With the motor running, slowly add ¼ cup water, gradually adding up to ¼ cup more until the dressing reaches your desired thickness and consistency. Transfer the dressing to a sealable jar, and chill in the refrigerator.

3   Make the breaded tomatillos: Cut the tomatillos in half, crosswise. In a small bowl, combine the flour with the salt and pepper.

4   Place the beaten egg and panko in two separate small bowls. Dredge each tomatillo half in the flour, dip it into the beaten egg, and then bathe it in the panko crumbs. Transfer the breaded tomatillos to a large plate or tray.

5   In a medium-hot skillet, heat the butter and olive oil. Let the butter brown and bubble slightly. Fry the breaded tomatillos, in batches, turning them with tongs until all sides are crispy and golden brown. Be sure not to overcrowd the skillet. Transfer to a paper towel–lined plate or tray and sprinkle with additional sea salt while warm.

6   Combine the salad components: Place the shredded kale in a large bowl. Gradually add the dressing until the leaves are coated and toss to combine. Add the avocado slices or scoops into the salad. Nest the breaded tomatillos in the greenery. Season with more salt and pepper, if desired.

7   Serve immediately, with a small vessel of additional green goddess dressing at the table.

Frida Kale-o Salad

Maxwell Fry-Up

Maxwell Fry-Up

Serves 2

It was a late night. You were out drinking at the Isokon Flats's Isobar, and had one too many. But now it's Saturday morning. Your wife, the acclaimed architect Jane Drew, is in the other room looking over the construction drawings for your next building. And it's your turn to make breakfast. The drum circle in your frontal cortex and grumbling stomach need you to come up with an idea fast. The solution? Why, a Maxwell Fry-Up, of course. A stir-fry meets a fry-up, this dish is an economical use of the limited footprint provided by the surface of your skillet. Timed wisely, it is also an economical use of your limited patience. Like the principles of building, it is premised on the concept of "vertical cooking," adding elements, according to their density and mass, that require less heat as you go.

3–4 strips	applewood-smoked bacon
3 small	potatoes, scrubbed
1 small	onion
1–2	scallions
1–2 cloves	garlic
1	jalapeño or red chile pepper
1	tomato
½ 15-ounce can (425 g)	navy or great Northern beans, rinsed and drained

2	tbsp	tomato paste
2	tbsp	ketchup
1	tsp	Worcestershire sauce
1	tsp	red wine vinegar
to	taste	kosher salt and black pepper
1	bunch (6 to 8 ounces/168 to 218 g)	broccolini, ends trimmed
¼	cup	fresh cilantro leaves or parsley leaves
2–3		precooked beets
1		avocado, sliced
¼	cup (57 g)	plain Greek, sheep's, or goat's milk yogurt (optional)

Steps

1 Season the skillet: Start with a firm foundation by placing strips of applewood-smoked bacon in a large cast-iron skillet over medium heat. Let the bacon fat start to render, reducing the heat to medium-low if it begins to splatter.

2   Prepare the potatoes: Quarter the potatoes, then place in a small pot filled with water. Cover, bring the water to a boil, and parboil the potatoes for 10 minutes. When ready, you should be able to insert the prongs of a fork into the potatoes' flesh, but the potatoes should not be mealy. Drain well and set aside.

3   Keep an eye on the bacon while you prepare the vegetables: Chop the onion into large dice. Slice the scallions. Mince the garlic cloves. Seed and finely chop the jalapeño or red chile pepper. Halve the tomato.

4   Back to the bacon: Once browned and crispy, remove the bacon from the skillet and transfer to a paper towel–lined plate. Leave the remaining bacon fat in the skillet.

5   Baked beans cheat: In a bowl, combine half a drained can of navy or great Northern beans with the tomato paste, ketchup, Worcestershire sauce, and red wine vinegar. Set aside.

6   Cook the potatoes: In the skillet with the bacon grease over medium-low heat, carefully place the drained potatoes, leaving a little bit of space around them so the heat has room to circulate to ensure crisping. Be careful, as the heat from the potatoes may cause grease to splatter.

7   Gradually increase the heat to medium. Try not to move the potatoes too much so that they begin to brown. After a few minutes add the onion and garlic. Season with salt and pepper. Cook, stirring occasionally, until the onion softens and becomes translucent. At this point, the potatoes should be getting some color. They are now going to act as a wall or partition device.

8   Add greenery: On one side of the skillet, add the broccolini to cook in the bacon grease. Cook the broccolini until the stalks and leaves begin to char, just a few minutes. Meanwhile, flip the potatoes so their sides are evenly browned.

9   Add your baked beans: On the other side of the potato partition, cook the baked bean mixture. Let the ketchup and tomato paste caramelize; allow them to commingle with bits of the onion and garlic from the potatoes so the aromatics can perform double duty. After a few minutes, the beans will be cooked through and their sauce will thicken.

Continued

Maxwell Fry-Up

10   Move the bean mixture to the side, so it occupies a quarter of the pan. As you attend to cooking the remaining ingredients, keep an eye on the beans as the tomato sauce can over-reduce and burn. Give them a gentle stir once in a while.

11   Add your accoutrements: Add tomato halves, cut side down, beside the beans. Let the tomato char before turning it over. Adjust seasoning, adding salt and pepper if necessary. Sprinkle sliced scallions and cilantro leaves or parsley atop the potatoes. Serve with precooked beets, sliced avocado, and a dollop of yogurt, if desired. Then go back to bed.

Shigeru Banchan Two Ways

Shigeru Banchan Two Ways

Serves 4 to 6

Recycled cardboard tubes may seem like an unlikely material for architecture. But for Japanese architect Shigeru Ban, who first demonstrated their use in the design of emergency shelters, paper has been the basis of his expanding lexicon of architectural works. The architect's privileging of resourcefulness over resources is an ethos that is shared, on culinary terms, by the Korean *banchan*. As small side dishes, banchan are served in the middle of a table for guests to share. They typically showcase a range of cooking techniques applied to a handful of basic ingredients, revealing the vast possibilities of what vegetables can do. Inspired by Shigeru Ban's paper tubes, this recipe takes the lowly cucumber (*oi*, in Korean) as its protagonist. Spiced, salted, and sautéed, two recipes for oi salute finding the means to create in the midst of perceived lack.

For the spicy cucumber salad *(oi muchim)*

4–5		Kirby or Persian cucumbers, or 1 English cucumber
1		scallion, sliced
2	tbsp	soy sauce
1	tsp	granulated sugar
1	tbsp	Korean red chile flakes *(gochugaru)*
1	tbsp	sesame seeds
1½	tsp	toasted sesame oil

Steps

1   Quarter the cucumbers lengthwise and cut into 1-inch (2.5 cm) pieces.

2   In a bowl, toss the cucumbers with the remaining ingredients.
Serve immediately or store in an airtight container in the refrigerator for a few days.

For the stir-fried cucumbers *(oi bokkeum)*

4–5	Persian cucumbers, or 1 English cucumber (1 pound)
1½ tsp	kosher salt
2 tsp	neutral-flavored oil
1 tsp	pure sesame oil
1 tsp	sesame seeds

Steps

1   Slice the cucumbers into thin disks. In a bowl, salt the cucumbers. Let them sit for 20 minutes, then squeeze the cucumbers to draw out the moisture, discarding any liquid.

2   In a skillet, heat the oil over medium heat. Sauté the salted cucumbers until they wilt, a few minutes or so. Remove from the heat.

3   Stir in the sesame oil and sesame seeds. Serve immediately.

Vladimir Tarte Tatlin

Vladimir Tarte Tatlin

Makes 12 tarts

Tatlin's Tower (1919–20) was a Constructivist symbol of innovation, designed by the avant-garde Soviet architect and artist Vladimir Tatlin. A soaring monument to modernity, it was to be built from iron, glass, and steel—industrial materials regarded, in the early twentieth century, as markers of great technological power and progress. It's dubious as to whether the altitudinous double-helical structure could have actually stood. Still, despite its precariousness, this recipe for tomato tarte Tatin applauds Tatlin's courageous and utopian aspirations, rather than critique the cataclysmic debacle that would have ensued. Sticky, caramelized onion and roasted tomato tarts are stacked high in a gravity-defying presentation. Yet rather than worry about their topsy-turvy demise, fear not—for these delectable treats will surely be consumed by your guests before any imminent collapse.

For the tomatoes

6		plum tomatoes, each roughly the diameter of an individual muffin
¾	tsp	kosher salt
¼	tsp	black pepper

For the caramelized onions

1	tbsp (15 g)	butter
2	tsp	olive oil
2		onions, thinly sliced
1½	tsp	red wine vinegar

For the caramel

4	tbsp	light brown sugar
2	tbsp (30 g)	butter
2	tsp	fresh thyme leaves

1	sheet	puff pastry, thawed and cut into 12 rounds using a cookie cutter

---

Steps

1   Prepare the tomatoes: Preheat the oven to 275°F (140°C). Halve the tomatoes crosswise and sprinkle with salt and pepper. In a 12-cup muffin tin, place prepared tomato halves, arranging them face up in the individual cups. Roast until skins are wrinkly, 2 hours. Set aside.

2   While the tomatoes roast, cook the onions: In a skillet, heat the butter and oil over medium-low heat. Caramelize the onions until soft, browned, and tender. Deglaze the pan with red wine vinegar.

3   Make the caramel: In a separate saucepan, heat the light brown sugar and butter over medium-low heat until a sticky, light caramel forms. Butter a clean 12-cup muffin tin, then pour the caramel into the cups, distributing the mixture evenly.

4   Mobilize the tart revolution: Increase the oven temperature to 425°F (220°C). To assemble each tart, sprinkle a few thyme leaves atop the pools of caramel. Place a dried tomato half, cut side down, in each muffin cup and add a spoonful of caramelized onions. Top with a round of puff pastry, tucking the edges into the cup. Bake until the pastry is golden, 20 to 25 minutes. Let cool for a few minutes in the tin.

5   Carefully invert the tin onto a board and leave it for a minute or two, allowing gravity to release the tarts and their sticky caramel. Let cool and stack the gooey tarts as high as they will go.

Vladimir Tarte Tatlin

Rosalind Sauerkrauss

Rosalind Sauerkrauss

Makes 1 to 1½ quarts (1 to 1.4 l)

For the art historian Rosalind Krauss, formlessness was a strategy used by artists to allow creative practice to engage with the everyday—to enable the detritus of life to seep into the realization of the artwork itself. Spoiled and soiled, tarnished and entropic, the breaking down of form was a technique to erode boundaries, categories, and distinctions. Lacto-fermentation, then, must surely be the culinary equivalent to the process of *l'informe* that Krauss so eloquently theorized. As an act of self-administered spoilage, it encourages bacteria in the atmosphere to decompose the integrity of plant matter, producing a distinctive funk that marks the contact zone between our bodies and our microbial counterparts. Consider this sauerkraut, then, a strategy of moving from sour sublation to sublimation—as figure and ground, cabbage and bacteria collapse to produce a new synthesis that moves the condiment closer to the edge of digestibility.

1 medium	head of cabbage
	(approx. 3 pounds/1.4 kg)
1½ tbsp	kosher salt
	plus 1 tsp to dissolve in the brine
1 tbsp	caraway seeds
–	Sanitized glass jar
–	Cheesecloth

Steps

1   Wash the cabbage well. Core and thinly slice.

Continued

László Macaroni-Nagy

László Macaroni-Nagy

Serves 4 to 6

Imagine poor Moholy after a long day of lecturing at the Bauhaus. He even spent hours in the darkroom to make some photograms afterward. With a grumbling, empty stomach (fasting spurred by Johannes Itten's intolerable garlic regimen at the Bauhaus cafeteria), who could fault him for wanting comfort food? Like a hug in a bowl (though, let's face it: modernists rarely showed emotion), this recipe for Hungarian macaroni and cheese *(túrós csusza)* is Constructivist pasta at its finest. Four basic ingredients and a pot produce a basic structure that can be easily customized: add bacon, caramelized onions, some chives, or don't. This is the ABCs of dinner.

1 16-ounce package (454 g)	wide egg noodles
3 to 4 strips	smoky bacon, diced
1 clove	garlic, minced
2 cups (454 g)	plain yogurt (or sour cream), plus more to taste
1½ cups (340 g)	cottage cheese, plus more to taste
to taste	Kosher salt and black pepper
	Smoked paprika

Steps

1   In a large pot of boiling salted water, cook the noodles until al dente (1 to 2 minutes short of indicated time, usually about 8 minutes). Drain the noodles.

2   In a skillet, sauté the diced bacon over medium heat until medium crispy. Transfer the bacon to a paper towel–lined plate. Set aside.

3   In the skillet with the bacon fat, fry the noodles until their edges become crispy. Add the minced garlic, making sure not to burn it.

4   Working quickly, add dollops of yogurt (or sour cream) and cottage cheese to the noodles. Carefully flip the noodles without breaking them. The cottage cheese will start to bubble and melt. Season with salt and pepper.

5   Transfer to a large serving platter. Add more dollops of yogurt and cottage cheese. Sprinkle the pasta with bacon and a dusting of paprika. Serve with side of steamed greens or baby broccoli.

László Macaroni-Nagy

Lucy Orta Torta

Lucy Orta Torta

Serves 6 to 8

Lucy Orta's tent-like, inhabitable sculptures are the inspiration for this torta, in which a sheet of flaky pastry forms the architectural covering for a mound of savory filling. Inside, networks of sautéed vegetables and cheese commingle to produce a dense and richly satisfying pie. Flexible and adaptable, held together through the elastic framework of dough, virtually any combination of vegetables or meat can be substituted in this dish. Experiment with creating irregular shapes, adorn it with pastry patterns, or aggregate it into smaller, self-contained packages. Regardless of what route you take, it travels and reheats well, making it the perfect supper for any nomad.

For the pastry

3	cups (360 g)	unbleached all-purpose flour, plus more for dusting
1	tsp	kosher salt
¾	cup (1½ sticks/170 g)	unsalted butter, cubed and cold
1	large	egg, beaten

For the filling

3	tbsp	olive oil
4	cups (300 g)	cremini mushrooms, sliced
1	medium	onion, sliced
4	tbsp	fresh herbs such as thyme or sage, minced
2	cloves	garlic, minced
1½	tsp	kosher salt

Yayoi Kusama Pumpkin Mochi

Yayoi Kusama Pumpkin Mochi

Makes 15 mochi

Yayoi Kusama's ovular obsession forms the basis for this mochi recipe, which replicates a pouch-like motif into infinity. Inside the space-age-spotted *daifuku* is a soft orange center of pumpkin, white chocolate, and salted caramel. Yet its polka-dot exterior has an unexpected crunch from crisped rice coated in white chocolate. Consuming this whimsical mochi, an unusual approach to a much-loved treat, is a form of repetition that you will surely not tire of.

For the pumpkin filling

⅓	cup	(56 g)	white chocolate chips
⅓	cup	(56 g)	salted caramel chips
1	tbsp		heavy cream
⅔	cup	(150 g)	canned pumpkin purée
¼	tsp		ground cinnamon

For the mochi dough

—			Potato starch, for dusting
1	cup	(150 g)	shiratamako or mochiko flour
¾	cup	(150 g)	granulated sugar

—	White Callebaut Crispearls, for decorating

Steps

1   In a medium heat-proof bowl, combine the white chocolate, salted caramel, and heavy cream. In a small saucepan, bring 2 inches (5 cm) of water to a simmer over medium-low heat. Place the bowl over the saucepan, making sure the bowl does not make direct contact with the water. Stir occasionally to melt the chocolate and salted caramel.

2   Add the pumpkin and cinnamon and cook, stirring the mixture occasionally, until most of the water in the pumpkin has evaporated, roughly 20 minutes. The mixture will reduce. Remove the bowl from the heat, and let it cool to room temperature. Chill, covered, in the refrigerator until the filling becomes thicker and amenable to scooping.

3   Meanwhile, dust a rimmed baking sheet or large dish with potato starch. In a small saucepan, whisk the shiratamako or mochiko flour with 1⅓ cups (320 ml) water. Set the saucepan over medium-low heat. Add the sugar. With a wooden spoon or spatula, cook the mixture, stirring constantly, until it thickens and comes together into a glossy, loose dough, roughly 5 to 8 minutes. Be careful that you don't burn or brown the dough.

4   Tip the dough onto the dusted baking sheet, then let the dough cool. Cut the dough into 15 pieces. Use your fingers to stretch each piece into a small disk. Place 1 small teaspoon of filling in the center of each disk. Stretch the dough around the filling, pinching it shut at one end. Then use your hands to shape the delicate mochi into a circle. Place it on a tray lined with parchment paper.

5   With moist hands, take each daifuku, and press the ball into a small cup containing the Crispearls. (The moisture from your hands will remove any potato starch on the daifuku allowing the Crispearls to stick. Too much water will prevent them from sticking.) Once the daifuku are coated, gently place them back on the tray. Freeze for several hours until they are firm. Eat them the same day or store them in an airtight container in the refrigerator for a few days.

Yayoi Kusama Pumpkin Mochi

Hélio Oiticica Stuffed
Parangolés

Hélio Oiticica Stuffed *Parangolés*

Makes 18 dumplings

Brazilian artist Hélio Oiticica's *Parangolés* (1964–79) were colorful, tent-like structures, made out of fabric, that were worn by dancing participants to produce a moving architecture of the body. Like abstract compositions, these "habitable paintings" were buoyant and free-flowing demarcations of the energy of people, and of life, that could be worn by anyone. Producing fluid shapes and sizes, *Parangolés* were, at once, entirely subjective, directed by the whims of an individual, and collective, as bodies moved in unison to the beat of a samba tune. Likewise, this edible interpretation of Oiticica's restless wrapper takes the form of a colored dumpling—a universal foodstuff that traverses cultures and geographies. As a mash-up between a Bolivian salteña, Japanese gyoza, Chinese soup dumpling, and the global form of the empanada, these stuffed parangolés are a reminder of what unites us, irrespective of the cloaks and colors we may inhabit.

For the filling

—		Neutral-flavored oil
1	pound (454 g)	ground beef or stewing beef, cut into small pieces
1		onion, finely diced
2	cloves	garlic, minced
2	tbsp	Korean hot pepper paste *(gochujang)* or *ají panca*
1	tsp	ground cumin
2	tsp	paprika
1	tbsp	dried oregano
1	cup (240 ml)	bone broth (see p. 30)
1	small	potato, peeled and finely diced
½	cup (90 g)	golden raisins

132, 133

to taste	kosher salt and black pepper
½ cup (100 g)	frozen peas
18	black olives, pitted and halved

For the pastry

1 cup (2 sticks/230 g)	unsalted butter
2 tsp	annatto powder, ground turmeric, or beet powder, sifted (for color)
¼ cup (50 g)	granulated sugar
2 tsp	kosher salt
3¾ cups (454 g)	unbleached all-purpose flour, plus more for dusting
1	egg white, for brushing

Steps

1   Make the filling: In a large skillet, heat the oil over medium heat. Sauté the beef until it begins to brown. Add the diced onion, garlic, and hot pepper paste, and cook until the onion turns translucent. Push the mixture to the side, and add the cumin, paprika, and oregano to the skillet, letting the spices cook in the oil for a minute or two before incorporating with other skillet ingredients. Add ½ cup of bone broth, diced potatoes, and raisins. Season with salt and pepper. Reduce heat to low.

2   Cover and simmer until the beef is cooked through and potatoes are tender, 30 minutes. Add the remaining ½ cup of broth. In the last 5 minutes of cooking, add the frozen peas.

3   Remove the skillet from the heat, and let the filling cool to room temperature. Chill in the refrigerator, covered, until the filling has solidified, roughly 3 to 4 hours, or 2 hours in the freezer. The broth should congeal into a golden jelly.

4   Make the pastry: In a medium saucepan, melt the butter and annatto (or turmeric or beet powder) over medium-low heat to infuse the butter with color. In a second saucepan, dissolve the sugar and salt in ¾ cup boiling water.

5   Place the flour in a large mixing bowl. Add the melted butter to the flour. Mix with a wooden spoon until combined. Stir ¾ cup (180 ml) hot water into the flour mixture. Knead until the dough forms a ball, adding more water gradually if the mixture seems dry. The dough should be slightly glossy, smooth, and pliable.

6   Divide the dough into 9 portions. Wrap the dough with plastic wrap and chill in the refrigerator for 30 minutes.

7   Assemble the pastries: Line a rimmed baking sheet with parchment paper. Subdivide the 9 portions of dough in half, so you have 18 golf ball–sized pieces in total. Work with 1 portion at a time. Keep the unused dough covered to prevent it from drying out.

8   Take a ball and press it into a disk. Using a rolling pin on a lightly floured surface, roll out the disk into a 5-inch (13 cm) shape (oval, circle, triangle, or rectangle). Place 2 tablespoons of the chilled filling into the center, followed by 2 olive halves. Fold the dough in half, pinching and crimping the edges to seal the parcel into your desired shape. Be inventive.

9   Transfer the dumpling to the lined baking sheet. Continue with the remaining dough and filling until 18 pastries are formed. Freeze the pastry parcels for at least 1 hour.

10 Bake the pastries: Preheat the oven to 450°F (230°C). Place the frozen pastries on a lightly oiled parchment-lined baking sheet. Brush the pastries with egg white for a shiny crust. Bake until golden brown, about 20 minutes.

Hélio Oiticica Stuffed *Parangolés*

Yokonomiyaki

Yokonomiyaki

Serves 4 to 6

In Yoko Ono's 1964 performance *Cut Piece*, participants approached the seated artist, adorned in her best suit, and proceeded to cut portions of her garment off with a pair of scissors. In accordance with the "score," a set of instructions written by the artist, participants could keep the portion of the garment they had cut. Whereas, for Ono, *Cut Piece* was largely a study of how much people will choose to take, "the cut" in this *okonomi* recipe performs as an act leading to amassment, adornment, and sharing. A giant pancake is created, magically, by combining threads of elastic batter that hold together mounds of shredded cabbage. Once fried, the crispy mound is further decorated with fragments of ginger, seaweed, bonito, and tempura bits. Served communally with scissors, guests are encouraged to snip portions of the pancake to serve to others, rather than for themselves.

For the pancake batter

1	cup	(120 g)	unbleached all-purpose flour
¼	tsp		kosher salt
¼	tsp		baking powder
¾	cup	(180 ml)	dashi stock
1	3-inch	(8 cm)	*nagaimo* or *yamaimo* (mountain or Chinese yam), peeled and grated
4	cups	(370 g)	green cabbage (about ½ a small head), thinly sliced
4	tbsp		dried bonito flakes
2	large		eggs, beaten
½	cup	(13 g)	*tenkasu* (tempura scraps)
1	tbsp	(15 g)	unsalted butter or neutral oil

Richard Diebeinkorn Bread

Richard Diebeinkorn Bread

Makes 1 round loaf

American painter Richard Diebenkorn often spoke about the trials of painting, which echo those of bread making. The problem presented by a blank canvas was not something he enjoyed. But the act of return, of working through struggles, was a necessary part of creation. Just as Diebenkorn relished a painting's anomalies, the task of bread making asks you to embrace its imperfections. Experiment with using different ratios of water, inserting herbs or spices, and baking in unconventional vessels. Don't be held back by perfection; embrace the ambiguity and unpredictable nature of the endeavor.

3	tsp	dry yeast
4	tsp	olive oil
2	tbsp	honey
6	cups (720 g)	all-purpose einkorn flour
2	tsp	sea salt

Steps

1   Butter an 8-inch (20 cm) cast-iron pot. In a large bowl, stir yeast with olive oil, honey, and 3 cups (720 ml) warm water.

2   Add the flour to the wet mixture. Sprinkle with the salt. Mix with a spatula until the flour is incorporated. The dough will be very sticky.

3   Transfer the dough to the greased cast-iron pot and cover with greased plastic wrap to avoid sticking. Let the dough proof in the pot for 30 minutes. Preheat the oven to 375°F (190°C).

4   Remove the plastic wrap and bake for 40 minutes. Let it cool before slicing.

M
A
I
N
S

Superstewdio

Superstewdio

Serves 4

Peposo was a peppery beef stew invented by Brunelleschi's laborers during the building of the Florence Cathedral in the fifteenth century. The builders slow-cooked inexpensive cuts of meat and red wine in the kilns they used to produce tiles for the building. Cobbling their resources together, a healthy pile of black pepper and a sprig of rosemary were all that was available to flavor the dish, but it was all that was needed. After a day's work, the hearty stew was shared in solidarity among the workers. This version of peposo translates their recipe as a tribute to Superstudio, the radical sixties architectural collective, also from Florence, who reinterpreted Brunelleschi's penchant for tiles into endless, monumental proportions. Zooming into the future, the subtle additions of garlic and tomato create a stew that acts as a contemporary reminder of the power of coming together to realize a common goal.

2	tbsp	olive oil
2 pounds (908 g)		stewing beef such as beef shin or beef shank, cubed
to taste		kosher salt and black pepper
½	head	garlic, peeled, cloves smashed
1½	cups (360 ml)	Chianti or dry red wine
1	cup (240 ml)	bone broth (see p. 30), or water

4	tbsp	tomato paste
2	sprigs	fresh rosemary
1		bay leaf
2	tbsp	coarsely ground black pepper

Steps

1   In a medium cast-iron pot, heat the olive oil over medium-high heat. Season the beef cubes with salt and pepper, then sear in the pot, being careful not to move them too much so a beautiful brown crust forms.

2   Turn the beef cubes to brown the other side for a few minutes. If the pot is overcrowded, brown the beef in batches, making sure to reserve any juices that are released on the plate while resting. Add the garlic to the pot and cook for a few minutes, then return the beef and the juices (if cooked in batches) to the pot.

3   Deglaze the pot with two-thirds of the red wine, scraping the fond off the bottom of the pot. Let the wine reduce slightly for a few minutes. Add the bone broth and the tomato paste, stirring to dissolve. Add the rosemary and bay leaf and bring this mixture to a boil. Once it is bubbling, cover the pot, and reduce the heat to a low simmer for 2½ hours.

4   Add the remaining one-third of the red wine and season with the coarsely ground black pepper. Simmer for an additional 30 minutes.

5   Remove the bay leaf and rosemary sprigs. You can serve it now, but the flavor will improve if refrigerated overnight and reheated. Chilling the stew will cause the fat to separate and rise to the top; this should be skimmed off with a spoon before reheating. Enjoy in ceramic bowls with crusty bread or polenta, and good company.

Jackson Pollock Pot Pie

Jackson Pollock Pot Pie

Serves 6

A fisherman's house and its barn in Long Island, New York, became the place of residence and studios for Jackson Pollock and Lee Krasner in 1945. In tribute to East Hampton's cookery, this pot pie features pollock, a humble fish that at one time swam aplenty in the Atlantic, but you could also substitute cod or haddock. This velvety stew comprising a medley of shellfish and aromatic vegetables is punctuated with the liquid paint of hot sauce splattered spontaneously atop abstract shards of puff pastry. When deconstructed on a plate, its various components—sautéed, strewn, and splintered—reveal a synthetic composition that is at once texturally dynamic and richly comforting.

For the shrimp stock

—		Shells from ½ pound shrimp used below
1 to 2 tbsp		fish sauce

For the pollock pot pie

1	pound (454 g)	pollock or cod fillets
½	pound (227 g)	raw shrimp
⅓	pound (150 g)	raw scallops
2–3	small	potatoes, scrubbed and quartered
1	tbsp (15 g)	butter
2	tbsp	olive oil
1		onion, finely diced
1		leek, thinly sliced
1		carrot, finely diced
1		fennel bulb, thinly sliced

2	cloves	garlic, _{minced}
1		bay leaf
1	sprig	fresh thyme
½	tsp	kosher salt
¼	tsp	black pepper
6	tbsp (45 g)	unbleached all-purpose flour, plus more for dusting

4	cups (960 ml)	shrimp stock

–		Splash of Pernod

4	tbsp	chopped fresh parsley

½	cup (120 ml)	whole milk or half-and-half, warmed

¼	tsp	Old Bay seasoning

⅛	tsp	cayenne pepper

1	sheet	frozen puff pastry, thawed

1		egg, beaten

For the garnish

–		Hot sauce
–		Fresh parsley, chopped

Steps

1   Make the shrimp stock: Peel and devein the shrimp, reserving the shells. Set the shrimp aside and refrigerate until ready to assemble the pie. In a medium pot, combine the shrimp shells with 1.5 quarts (1.4 l) water and bring to a boil. Reduce the heat to a low rolling boil and cook for 15 to 20 minutes. Add the fish sauce.

2   Prepare the seafood: Check the fish fillets for bones, removing any with tweezers. Remove the skin and cube the fish into 2-inch (5 cm) chunks. Cut the scallops in half if large so they are approximately the same size as the chunks of fish. Keep the seafood refrigerated until ready to use.

3   Make the seafood stew: In a small pot, parboil the potatoes until fork-tender but still firm. Rinse under cold water and drain well.

4   In a stockpot, heat the butter and olive oil. Add the onion, leek, carrot, and fennel and cook until softened. Add the minced garlic, bay leaf, thyme, salt, and pepper, and cook for a few minutes. Add the flour, stirring gently, and cook for a few minutes more.

5   Gradually add the shrimp stock to the pot, one ladle at a time, while stirring constantly. Reduce the heat to low and let the stew simmer until the broth thickens, about 10 minutes. Adjust the seasoning, adding salt and pepper, if needed. Add a splash of Pernod and parsley, and stir in the warmed milk (or half-and-half), Old Bay seasoning, and cayenne. Cook until the stew thickens and becomes creamy, 5 to 10 minutes more.

6   Assemble the pie: Preheat the oven to 375°F (190°C). In a 9 x 13-inch (23 x 33 cm) casserole or baking dish, evenly distribute the chunks of fish fillet, shrimp, and scallops. Slowly pour the seafood stew atop the seafood pieces.

7   On a lightly floured surface, roll out the puff pastry into a rectangle that is slightly larger than the casserole dish. Cut the pastry dough into angular shards, letting spontaneity guide you. Place the shards of puff pastry atop the seafood stew and brush with beaten egg. Bake the pot pie until the puff pastry is golden brown, 35 to 40 minutes. To serve, have hot sauce and additional parsley at the table, which guests can scatter over their portions.

Jackson Pollock Pot Pie

Robert   Rauschenburger

Robert Rauschenburger

Serves 4

Robert Rauschenberg was a fan of scraps. The artist scanned the streets of New York collecting them for use in his combines. But his fondness for the fragmentary also informed his approach to cooking, using ingredients that were readily on hand. This burger recipe is inspired by Rauschenberg's penchant for leftovers. A juicy hamburger patty is treated as a large surface onto which numerous toppings can be added, akin to what art historian Leo Steinberg referred to as "a flatbed picture plane." Resulting in wild and sometimes incompatible juxtapositions, the dish transforms culinary composition into a communal activity of collage.

1	pound (454 g)	good-quality ground beef
¼	tsp	kosher or sea salt
⅛	tsp	black pepper
–		Olive oil
3	tsp	yellow mustard
1	large	focaccia, roughly 9 x 12 inches (23 x 30 cm)
–		Various burger toppings

Steps

1   Heat a grill, or if using a stove, a large grill pan, to high heat.
     Season the meat with salt and pepper. On a tray, shape the beef into
     a rectangle, roughly 7 x 10 inches (18 x 25 cm), slightly smaller than
     your focaccia. Lightly brush the olive oil on both sides of the meat.

2   Sear the burger on one side for a few minutes. While it cooks, glaze the
     side facing up with half of the yellow mustard. Carefully flip the burger
     and sear the other side. Glaze this side of the patty with the remaining
     yellow mustard. The beef should have a crisp, browned exterior.

3   Meanwhile, preheat the oven to 350°F (180°C). Place the focaccia on a
     baking sheet and warm in the oven.

4   Place the patty on the warmed focaccia. Let your guests garnish with
     various toppings on the table. Cut and serve.

Robert Rauschenburger

Carolee Schneemann *Meat Joy*
Balls

Carolee Schneemann *Meat Joy* Balls

Serves 6

Meat Joy, Carolee Schneemann's seminal 1964 performance involved a group of naked dancers whose bodies were entangled in a sensual orgy with cuts of raw meat. Visceral and lush, like Schneemann's original event, this one-platter meal celebrates diversity by allowing contrasting and distinctive ingredients to intertwine. *Meat Joy* balls are a delight to craft and assemble, but they're even more of a thrill to consume. Just imagine slovenly layers of glossy vegetables, thickly slicked with olive oil and dollops of lemony herbed sheep's milk yogurt, mixed with a medley of aromatic lamb kefta perfumed with spices. The strata is tumbled onto mountains of couscous. Textures and flavors meld together harmoniously while also delivering a surprise in every bite. A hedonistic pleasure for both your eyes and taste buds.

For the couscous

1½ cups	(225 g)	couscous
1 tbsp		olive oil
pinch		kosher salt

For the roasted vegetables

2	zucchini, cut lengthwise into ¼-inch-thick (7 mm) slices
12–15	ripe cherry tomatoes, left whole
2–3	red and yellow peppers, sliced
1	red onion, quartered

156, 157

¼	cup	(60 ml)	olive oil
to	taste		sea salt and black pepper

For the lamb kefta

⅓	cup	(45 g)	pine nuts
1	small		onion
4	tbsp		fresh parsley leaves or stems
4	tbsp		fresh cilantro leaves or stems
2	slices		sandwich bread, torn
1	pound	(454 g)	ground lamb
½	tsp		ground allspice
1	tsp		kosher salt
¼	tsp		black pepper
½	tsp		cayenne pepper
⅓	tsp		ground cinnamon

For the yogurt sauce

1	cup	(227 g)	sheep's milk yogurt or Greek yogurt
1–2	cloves		garlic, finely minced
2	tbsp		fresh mint, finely minced
½			lemon, juiced and zested
to	taste		sea salt and black pepper

Additional herbs and condiments

– Harissa
– Dukkah
– Sumac
– Fresh cilantro leaves
– Fresh mint leaves
– Fresh baby lovage leaves (or celery leaves)

Steps

1   Prepare the couscous: Place the couscous in a medium bowl. Drizzle the olive oil over and add a pinch of salt. Pour in 1½ cups (360 ml) boiling water and stir. Cover the bowl with a large plate, and let the couscous absorb the liquid for 5 minutes. Before serving, fluff the couscous with a fork.

2   Roast the vegetables: Preheat the oven to 350°F (180°C). On a rimmed baking sheet or pan, cover the vegetables with a nice slick of olive oil and evenly distribute them, making sure to leave space between the vegetables (otherwise they will steam rather than roast). Lightly dust with sea salt and black pepper and bake until the zucchini have caramelized and the tomatoes have burst, 35 to 40 minutes.

3   Next, make the kefta: In a small skillet, toast the pine nuts over low heat until aromatic and lightly browned, a few minutes. Let cool to room temperature. In a food processor, grind the pine nuts until a powder forms; they should not turn into a paste. Remove from the processor and set aside.

4   Next, use the food processor, or a knife, to finely mince the onions, parsley, and cilantro.

Continued

Carolee Schneemann *Meat Joy* Balls

5   Meanwhile, in a small bowl, soak the torn slices of bread in water until softened. Squeeze out the excess water from the bread and discard the liquid.

6   In a large bowl, mix the lamb with the pine nuts, minced herbs and aromatics, softened bread, allspice, salt, pepper, cayenne, and cinnamon. Ensure that the ingredients are evenly combined. Form the lamb into meatballs, using about 1½ tablespoons of mixture per meatball.

7   Transfer the meatballs to a rimmed baking sheet. The lamb will release quite a bit of fat, so there is no need to grease the sheet. Bake at 350°F (180°C) until the meatballs are nicely browned, 30 to 35 minutes

8   Prepare the herbed yogurt sauce: Combine the yogurt, 1 clove of garlic, and mint. (The courageous may want to add a second clove of garlic, but lovers beware.) Gradually add lemon juice to suit your taste and to help achieve desired consistency. Season with salt and pepper.

9   Time to layer: Carefully place piles of couscous onto a large platter. This will be the base. Lay the grilled vegetables and their juices atop the couscous. Then add the succulent meatballs and their glorious juices, followed by dollops of herbed yogurt. To subtly boost the flavor and texture, add small dots of harissa or a tiny scattering of dukkah and sumac around the heap.

10   A light dusting of cilantro, mint, and baby lovage leaves is the final step. To create an interesting interplay of textures, experiment with finely mincing some herbs, while leaving the prettier leaves whole. Serve this platter family style and watch the gastronomic orgy ensue.

David Ham Hockney Pea Soup

David Ham Hockney Pea Soup

Serves 8

Ham hocks and peas may not seem like the stuff of dreams. Yet the delectable sweetness of both, despite their modest stature, offers a lip-smacking treat sure to please any Pop fanatic. Like David Hockney's vibrant paintings, a verdant pool of pea purée surrounds a meaty broth of startling complexity. A reminder that even the most banal and unassuming ingredients can be seen in new ways, this dish asks you to consider how the beauty of ordinary things becomes clear when they are merely taken at face value.

For the ham hock stock

2 pounds (about 1 kg)	ham hocks
2	celery stalks
1	carrot
1	onion
1	bay leaf
handful	peppercorns

For the pea soup

3–4 tbsp (45 to 60 g)	unsalted butter
1 small	onion, chopped
1–2 tsp	sea salt
1 clove	garlic, minced
½ cup (120 ml)	dry white wine
1 16-ounce package (454 g)	frozen peas

| 2–3 tbsp | fresh mint leaves |
| to taste | salt and black pepper |

Steps

1   Make the ham hock stock: The night before, soak the ham hocks in a large pot of water in the refrigerator to remove their saltiness. Drain and rinse them well before use.

2   In a large stockpot, combine the ham hocks with the vegetables, bay leaf, peppercorns, and 8 cups of water. Bring to a boil. Reduce the heat and simmer for 3 to 4 hours.

3   Strain the liquid, reserving the hocks. Pull the meat and skin off the hocks. Reserve and set aside.

4   Make the pea soup: In a large stockpot, melt the butter. Add the onion and salt and sauté until soft. Add the garlic and cook for a minute or two more.

5   Deglaze the pot with white wine and let it reduce, until most of the liquid has evaporated. Add 5 cups of ham hock stock to the pot, and bring the mixture to a boil. Add the frozen peas, then reduce the heat and cook for 10 minutes. Add the mint leaves.

6   Transfer the soup in batches to a blender and purée until smooth, using caution when blending the hot liquid. Return soup to the pot set over low heat, and season with additional salt and black pepper, if desired. Add the ham hock pieces to the soup and serve immediately.

Angus Martin

Angus Martin

Serves 1 to 2

After graduating from Columbia University's Teachers College in 1942, Agnes Martin taught art to high school students while working as a tennis coach, a waitress, a baker's helper, and a dishwasher. "Whenever I was really starving I always washed dishes because I got closer to the food," she said. During a hiatus from painting, she traveled in a camper across the United States to New Mexico, where she designed and constructed buildings using traditional materials. She made her own adobe bricks from straw and mud, and moved large vigas in her truck. The repetitive process of making bricks with her own hands brought her back to painting, eventually resulting in the grids she is best known for. As suggested by Martin's winding path—from Saskatchewan to Vancouver, Los Angeles to New York, Cuba, Galisteo, and eventually, Taos—she was in search of an abstract feeling encapsulated in colors of light, horizon lines, a mountaintop, the lines of a brick wall. This steak tartare, composed of hand-cut bricks of beef, emerald cilantro, the golden sunrise of yolk, wheaty flecks of plantain, and a haze of chile spice, is an homage to Martin's love of the hand-rendered, the solitary, and the iterative—and the renewal that comes through the values bestowed in them.

½	pound (227 g)	beef tenderloin
½		shallot, finely minced
¼	tsp	kosher salt
¼	tsp	black pepper
¼	tsp	ancho chile or chipotle chile powder
1	tbsp	fresh cilantro, finely minced

2	tsp	Worcestershire sauce
1½	tsp	extra-virgin olive oil
2	tsp	red wine vinegar
½		lemon, juiced
1		egg yolk (optional)
3	tbsp	crushed plantain chips, plus more (whole) for serving

Steps

1 Chill the meat, placing it in the freezer briefly, to facilitate cutting.

2 With your sharpest knife, finely dice the tenderloin into small cubes.

3 In a bowl, gently combine the beef with the salt, pepper, chile powder, shallot, cilantro, and Worcestershire sauce. Drizzle the olive oil over the meat and mix gently to combine. Add the vinegar and lemon juice and combine again.

4 On a plate, place the raw egg yolk in the center, if using. Working quickly, arrange the cubes of seasoned tartare over the yolk to form a stacked wall or grid. Adorn the top of the tartare grid with crushed plantain chips. Serve immediately, with additional plantain chips.

Angus Martin

Andrea Branzini

Helen Frankfurtenthaler

Helen Frankfurtenthaler

Serves 6 to 8

American Abstract Expressionist painter Helen Frankenthaler developed an unusual and innovative technique known as the soak-stain method: She'd let thinned paint saturate an unprimed canvas on the floor, which she would further manipulate through rolling, pouring, and tilting. This became the pictorial ground upon which additional colors could be added. Taking Frankenthaler's approach as its cue, this dish elevates ordinary beans and frankfurters by reimagining the legume as both its paint and canvas. Thinned into a creamy, garlicky pool, a puddle of white bean purée forms the canvas upon which a savory tomato and bean stew is added in spontaneous dollops. With the addition of your favorite sausage, the composition is complete.

For the roasted garlic and white bean purée

1	pound (454 g)	dried great Northern, cannellini beans (or flageolet)
1	stalk	celery, halved
1	large	carrot, halved
2	cloves	garlic, peeled
½		white onion
1		bouquet garni (3 sprigs of fresh Italian parsley, 3 sprigs thyme, and 1 bay leaf)
–		Parmesan rind
2	tsp	kosher salt
½	tsp	black pepper, freshly ground
1	head	garlic, unpeeled
2	tsp	olive oil
1	tsp	red wine vinegar

For the bean and tomato stew

2	tbsp	olive oil
1½	large	onions, diced
2	large	carrots, diced
2	stalks	celery, diced
2	cloves	garlic, minced
2	tbsp	tomato paste
2	tsp	fresh thyme leaves
1	28-ounce can (794 g)	tomato purée
to	taste	kosher salt and black pepper

For the sausages

6–8		sausages
2	tbsp	fresh parsley leaves
1–2	tbsp	olive oil, for drizzling

Steps

1 Prepare the beans: In a large pot of cold water, place the beans, making sure they are submerged by 4 to 5 inches (10 to 12 cm). Cover and let them soak overnight.

2 Drain the beans and transfer to a large pot. Fill the pot with cold water, ensuring that the beans are covered by a few inches. Add the celery, carrot, garlic cloves, onion, and bouquet garni. Bring the mixture to a boil, then reduce heat to a simmer, stirring occasionally. Add the Parmesan rind after 30 minutes of cooking. Cook until the beans are tender, roughly 1 to 1½ hours.

3   Remove the vegetables, Parmesan rind, and herbs. Strain the mixture, reserving the cooking liquid. Reserve 4 cups of the beans for the purée, and 3 cups for the tomato stew. Keep the stock warm in a saucepan.

4   Roast a head of garlic: While the beans are cooking, preheat the oven to 400°F (200°C). Cut the top off an unpeeled head of garlic so its cloves peek out. Wrap the garlic in aluminum foil and roast in the oven for 40 minutes.

5   Make the bean and tomato stew: In a heavy-bottomed pot, heat 2 tablespoons of olive oil. Sauté the diced onions, carrots, and celery until soft but not browned. Add 2 minced garlic cloves and cook for a few minutes, then add tomato paste and thyme leaves and cook for a few more. Add the tomato purée, and season with salt and pepper. Cook until the sauce begins to thicken, 5 to 10 minutes.

6   Add 3 cups of the cooked beans. Cook until the beans are warmed through. Add some of the reserved bean stock to loosen if the mixture begins to thicken too much.

7   Make the roasted garlic and white bean purée: Using a food processor, purée 4 cups of cooked beans. Beginning with ½ cup, slowly ladle the reserved stock in gradual increments, while pulsing, until a creamy consistency is achieved. Squeeze the roasted garlic from the garlic skins into the processor. With the motor running, slowly drizzle 2 teaspoons olive oil and 1 teaspoon of red wine vinegar. Season with salt and pepper.

8   Fry the sausages: In a skillet, fry the sausages over medium heat until browned. Place a lid over the skillet for a few minutes while cooking to ensure they are cooked through.

9   Assemble the dish: Ladle a large platter with a puddle of bean purée. Tilt, smear, or spread the purée into a desired shape. Add splatters of the bean and tomato stew, creating unusual shapes. Place the sausages on top. Scatter parsley leaves over the composition, lightly drizzle with olive oil, and serve.

Helen Frankfurtenthaler

Yinka Shonibarebecue

Lawrence Weiners

Lawrence Weiners

Serves 8

(1) The artist may construct the weiner.
(2) The weiner may be purchased.
(3) The weiner need not be built.

Each being equal and consistent with the intent of the artist, the decision as to condition rests with the cook upon the occasion of cooking.

E.C.

1 14-ounce package (397 g)	hot dog weiners, aka "franks"
—	Ketchup or yellow mustard (optional)

Steps

1   Bring a medium pot of water to a boil over high heat.

2   Open the package of weiners and place them in the boiling water. Boil until plump, about 5 minutes.

3   Transfer to a dish and serve with ketchup or mustard.

D
E
S
S
E
R
T
S

Denise Scott Brownies

Denise Scott Brownies

Makes 14 to 16 cookies

The all-American brownie, devised in Boston in the early twentieth century, is a product of the vernacular and the quotidian, akin to the objects featured in Denise Scott Brown and Robert Venturi's taxonomy *Learning from Las Vegas* (1972). Yet as it turns out, cookies, not brownies, proved instrumental to forming Scott Brown's connection with Venturi. Indeed, it was Scott Brown's gesture of repeatedly saving a seat and a cookie for Venturi during University of Pennsylvania faculty meetings that facilitated their partnership—a testament to the power that a cookie can possess. As a wink to history, this recipe for Denise Scott Brownies adopts a cookie form. It features a subtle hint of smokiness from the unusual addition of black pepper—a nod to the pepper cookie popular in South Africa, where the architect pursued her studies—revealing a hidden complexity beneath its veneer of kitsch and panache.

1	cup (120 g)	unbleached all-purpose flour
½	cup (42 g)	Dutch-processed cocoa powder
½	tsp	baking soda
½	tsp	baking power
½	tsp	sea salt
⅛	tsp	black pepper
½ (1 stick/115 g)	cup	unsalted butter, at room temperature

½	cup (100 g)	granulated sugar
¾	cup (150 g)	coconut sugar or brown sugar
1½	tsp	pure vanilla extract
1	large	egg, at room temperature
6	ounces (170 g)	semisweet chocolate chips, preferably Guittard

Steps

1 Into a bowl, sift the flour, cocoa powder, baking soda, baking powder, salt, and pepper.

2 In a medium bowl, use an electric mixer set on low speed to cream the butter, sugar, coconut sugar, and vanilla for 3 minutes. Add the egg and beat on low speed for 15 seconds.

3 Add the sifted ingredients to the butter-egg mixture, gradually, beating on low speed until incorporated. Stir in the chocolate chips, then cover the bowl and chill the batter in the refrigerator for a minimum of 1 hour.

4 When ready to bake, preheat the oven to 350°F (180°C) and line a baking sheet with parchment paper or a silicone baking mat. Using a small ice-cream scoop or spoon, drop the chilled dough in heaping spoonfuls onto the lined baking sheet. Leave a 2-inch (5 cm) space between the cookies as they will spread. Bake for 11 to 13 minutes, keeping a close eye on them. For crispier cookies, increase the baking time by a few minutes. Keep the dough in the refrigerator between batches.

5 Carefully transfer the cookies to a wire rack. They will be soft but their exteriors will continue to firm and crisp as they cool. Embellish them with your most fabulous decorations. Remember: less is not more here.

Denise Scott Brownies

Michael Heizer *Levitated Mass*
Pavlova

Flan Flavin

Flan Flavin

Serves 10

This flan inspired by Dan Flavin's luminous fluorescent tube sculptures plays with the concept of "lightness" by offering an unexpected interplay of two subtly contrasting textural components. A featherweight whipped fluff of incandescent matcha cream sits atop a silky, beige filament of jiggly lime-infused flan. Best served as a serial line-up, this unassuming dessert is nothing short of an unconventional experiment in lambency for the tongue using prosaic grocery store materials—an experience that becomes more than the sum of its parts.

For the flan

2	cups	(480 ml)	whole milk
1	cup	(240 ml)	heavy cream
1½	cups	(297 g)	granulated sugar
3	strips		lime zest
⅛	tsp		sea salt
6	large		eggs
2	large		egg yolks
½	tsp		pure vanilla extract

For the matcha whipped cream

1½	cups	(360 ml)	heavy cream
1	tsp		culinary-grade matcha powder (or more to taste)
1–2 tsp			castor or superfine sugar (optional)

Steps

1   Preheat the oven to 325°F (165°C).

2   Prepare the flan: In a small saucepan, heat the milk, heavy cream, sugar, lime zest, and salt over low heat, stirring until the sugar has dissolved. Set aside.

3   In a blender, combine the eggs, egg yolks, and vanilla extract. Remove the lime zest from the hot milk mixture, and slowly pour the hot milk mixture into the blender with the motor running. Blend until smooth.

4   Pour the custard into a 9 x 5-inch (23 x 13 cm) loaf pan. Place the loaf pan into a larger baking dish. Pour hot water into the baking dish until it reaches halfway up the sides of the loaf pan. Bake it on an oven rack placed on the lower third of the oven until the flan slightly wobbles but is set, 45 minutes.

5   Carefully remove the loaf pan from the bain-marie. Avoid getting any water into your flan. Transfer the loaf pan to a wire rack to let cool for 30 minutes, then chill in the refrigerator for a minimum of 8 hours.

6   When ready to serve, remove the flan by running a knife around the edge of the loaf pan. Place a serving platter or dish over top the loaf pan and gently invert. You'll hear a plop when the flan decides to let go. Slice and arrange in uniform rows.

7   Make the matcha whipped cream: Using an electric mixer, whip the heavy cream in a bowl until soft peaks form. Add the matcha powder and continue to whip for another minute or two. The cream will taste slightly grassy, but the sweetness of the flan will offset it. However, you can add a bit of sugar, if desired.

8   Assembly: Dollop the emerald whipped cream atop the flan slices. Serve immediately.

Flan Flavin

Walter De Maria *Earth Room*
Chocolate Cake

Walter De Maria *Earth Room* Chocolate Cake

Serves 10 to 12

This chocolate cake is a celebration of the heady aroma and textures in the mantle of the earth that characterizes Walter De Maria's infamous installation, *Earth Room* (1977). Earth, mud, and soil are translated into a dense chocolate cake perfumed with chai spices, slathered with chocolate pudding, and topped with a thick sprinkle of edible chocolate crumbs. A veritable *Le Corbuffet* classic, the cake can be tiled to produce an endless field of chocolate terrain—a gratifying treat grounded in the pleasures of multi-sensory experience.

For the chocolate chai earth cake

2¼	cups (270 g)	unbleached all-purpose flour
¾	cup (64 g)	Dutch-processed cocoa powder
1¾	cup (347 g)	granulated sugar
1½	tsp	baking powder
½	tsp	baking soda
1	tsp	ground cinnamon
½	tsp	ground cardamom
¼	tsp	ground clove
¼	tsp	ground ginger
¼	tsp	ground nutmeg
½	tsp	kosher salt
½	cup	unsalted butter,

(1 stick/115 g)   at room temperature (plus more for greasing)

⅓	cup	(80 ml)	coconut oil
1	cup	(240 ml)	unsweetened almond milk, (preferably carrageenan-free)
2	tsp		pure vanilla extract
½	cup	(120 ml)	brewed coffee
4	large		eggs, at room temperature

For the chocolate mud pudding

½	cup	(100 g)	granulated sugar
4	tbsp		cornstarch
3	tbsp		Dutch-processed cocoa
pinch			sea salt
1¼	cups	(300 ml)	whole milk or coconut milk
⅓	cup	(2 ounces/57 g)	bittersweet chocolate (at least 70%), chopped
2	tbsp	(30 g)	unsalted butter, at room temperature
½	tsp		pure vanilla extract

For the chocolate soil

2¼	cups	(446 g)	granulated sugar
3	cups	(18 ounces/510 g)	chopped bittersweet chocolate (at least 70%)

Steps

1   Bake the earth cake: Preheat the oven to 350°F (180°C). Lightly butter a 9 x 13-inch (23 x 33 cm) rectangular baking dish and line the bottom with parchment paper.

2   Into the bowl of a stand mixer, sift the flour, cocoa powder, sugar, baking powder, baking soda, and spices. Add the butter and coconut oil to the dry ingredients, mixing on low speed. Add the almond milk, vanilla, and coffee and continue mixing on low speed for a couple of minutes.

3   Increasing the speed to medium, add the eggs, one at a time, mixing between additions, until incorporated.

4   Transfer the batter to the prepared cake pan and bake for 40 minutes, until a toothpick inserted into the center comes out clean. Remove cake from the oven and let it cool completely in the pan on a wire rack before removing.

5   Make the chocolate mud pudding: In a saucepan, cook the sugar, cornstarch, cocoa, salt, and milk over medium heat. Bring the mixture to a boil, stirring constantly. Add the chopped chocolate, stirring until melted and the pudding thickens. Remove the pudding from the heat and stir in the butter and vanilla. Let cool and chill, covered, in the refrigerator for about 30 to 40 minutes.

6   Make the chocolate soil: In a medium saucepan, place the sugar over low heat. Add ½ cup (120 ml) cold water and give the pot a gentle swirl. Try to avoid getting the sugar and water on the sides of the pot. Conjure all of your self-control to not stir this concoction. The sugar will begin to bubble and brown. At this point, remove the pot from the heat. Add the chopped chocolate while stirring continuously. It will immediately begin to look like soil. Transfer the soil to a sheet of parchment paper or a silicone baking mat and let cool.

7   Assemble the cake: Remove the parchment from the cooled chocolate cake. Place the cake on your serving platter and spread the chocolate mud pudding over it, concentrating it mostly on its top and sides. Finish with a sprinkling of chocolate soil, making sure the top and sides are thoroughly carpeted.

Walter De Maria *Earth Room* Chocolate Cake

Rem Brûlée

Rem Brûlée

Serves 6 to 8

When it comes to the work of Rem Koolhaas, what you see is not always what you get. Inspired by the architect who thrives on the unexpected, this grapefruit curd tart unites two dessert typologies—crème brûlée and a citrus tart—into a textural and toothsome medley, achieved through different layers of crunchy, velvety, and crumbly decadence. The best part of this dessert is that its silken interior can only be accessed by puncturing its sugary exterior, transforming the tart into a dialectical experience that is at once seductively sweet and critically acidic.

For the tart pastry

1½ cups	(195 g)	unbleached all-purpose flour, plus more for dusting
½ cup	(100g)	granulated sugar
¼ tsp		kosher salt
9 tbsp		unsalted butter, cubed and cold
(1 stick plus 1 tbsp/130 g)		
1 large		egg, beaten

For the grapefruit curd

1 large		ruby red grapefruit, finely zested and juiced
1 cup	(200 g)	granulated sugar
4 large		eggs
1⅓ cups		unsalted butter,
(2 sticks plus 5 tbsp/300 g)		cubed, at room temperature

For the brûlée topping

¼ cup (50 g)   granulated sugar

Steps

1   Prepare the tart pastry: In a food processor, combine the flour, sugar, and salt. Toss in the small cubes of butter. Pulse until the mixture resembles gravel. Gradually add the egg and continue to pulse until the dough begins to hold together.

2   Turn the dough onto a clean surface or large bowl and knead sparingly to make sure the ingredients are incorporated. Flatten into a disk, wrap in plastic wrap, and chill in the refrigerator for a minimum of 30 minutes and up to an hour.

3   Cut a circle of parchment to line the bottom of a 9-inch (23 cm) fluted tart pan with a removable bottom. Once the dough is chilled and rested, roll it out into a circle slightly larger than the circumference of the tart pan on a lightly floured surface. Carefully transfer the dough to the pan being careful to avoid stretching it. Gently press the dough into the pan's edges and sides. Glide the rolling pin over the pan to remove any overhang, and patch any cracks or holes with leftover dough. Chill the pastry in the refrigerator for a minimum of 2 hours.

4   Preheat the oven to 375°F (190°C), with the oven rack in the center position. Line the pastry with a sheet of foil fitted snugly around the crust, and add weights. Place the tart pan on a baking sheet and bake the dough for 25 to 30 minutes. Remove the foil and bake until golden brown, 5 to 10 minutes more. Transfer to a wire rack and let cool to room temperature.

5   Create the grapefruit curd: In a medium nonreactive bowl, mix the grapefruit zest with the sugar until grainy. Whisk in the grapefruit juice and eggs.

6   Place the bowl over a small saucepan filled with a few inches of simmering water. The water should not touch the bowl. Whisking constantly, cook the mixture over medium-low heat. Don't stop whisking—this will prevent the eggs from scrambling—but brace yourself, as you may need to whisk for upwards of 15 minutes.

7   The mixture will start to foam, form large bubbles, and eventually thicken. When the mixture reaches 180°F (82°C), there will be fewer bubbles and the cream will become a more uniformly thick surface. Remove the bowl from the heat and pass the mixture through a sieve into the jar of a blender. Let the filling cool to room temperature.

8   With the blender on high, add the butter to the filling, a few cubes at a time. Keep the motor whirring as all of the butter is incorporated, and let the mixture continue to aerate for an additional 4 to 5 minutes.

9   Assemble the tart: Pour the curd into the cooled tart shell, smoothing the top, and chill in the refrigerator for a minimum of 4 hours (or freeze, wrapped well, for 2 hours).

10 Add the brûlée topping: When it is time to serve, sprinkle a few spoons of sugar evenly over the tart filling. Use a kitchen torch to caramelize it into a molten crust. Let your guests have the pleasure of cracking the tart's top into shards at the table.

Dan Graham Crackers

Dan Graham Crackers

Serves 8 to 10

In *Rock My Religion* (1984), Dan Graham connected the history of American religious practices to the religious fervor of rock music and punk culture, examining both Shaker steps and mosh pits as communal attempts to attain transcendence. What better way, then, to commemorate our contemporary rituals of religiosity, than to nosh on a sweet wheat cracker devised to enact the divine will of God? Invented by Sylvester Graham, a fiery American Presbyterian minister, in 1829, graham crackers were part of a larger campaign to abolish the industrial use of refined flour. Advocating that the consumption of homemade, unsifted whole wheat flour would lead to temperance, he developed the graham cracker as a means to snack our way to moral reform. Assembled and consumed as s'mores, a nod to the artist's interest in childhood memory, use this dessert as an excuse to band together and applaud your piety.

For the graham crackers

1	cup	(113 g)	whole wheat flour
1	cup	(120 g)	unbleached all-purpose flour, plus more for dusting
¼	cup	(50 g)	granulated sugar
1½	tsp		ground cinnamon
1	tsp		baking powder
½	tsp		kosher salt or sea salt
¼	cup	(60 ml)	coconut oil
¼	cup	(85 g)	honey
3	tbsp		milk, plus more for glaze
1	large		egg

For the s'mores

1	cup (170 g)	bittersweet chocolate disks, preferably Guittard
1	10-ounce (285 g)	package vanilla marshmallows (approximately 40)

Steps

1   Make the graham crackers: In a large bowl, combine the (unsifted!) flours, sugar, cinnamon, baking powder, and salt. In a second bowl, whisk the coconut oil, honey, milk, and egg. Incorporate the wet mixture into the dry, until a dough forms. Wrap the dough with plastic wrap and chill in the refrigerator for 1 hour.

2   Preheat the oven to 300°F (150°C). Knead the dough until it becomes pliable, dividing it into 2 portions if it makes the process easier. On separate sheets of lightly floured parchment paper, roll out each portion until it is about the thickness of a coin.

3   Transfer the parchment with dough to 2 baking sheets. Brush the dough with milk, and add additional sugar or cinnamon, if desired. Bake for 10 minutes.

4   Remove the dough from the oven. Using a sharp knife or pastry cutter, score the dough into squares, leaving them connected. Return to the oven and bake until the crackers are nicely browned, 20 to 25 minutes more. Turn the oven off, then let the crackers cool in the oven, to ensure they crisp.

5   Make some s'mores: Preheat the oven to 350°F (180°C). To assemble a spread of s'mores, take 1 large sheet of graham crackers and place it on a baking sheet. Place a disk of chocolate on each graham cracker square, followed by a marshmallow. Carefully place the second sheet of graham crackers on top of the grid of standing marshmallows.

6   Bake it in the oven for 5 to 10 minutes, watching carefully that the marshmallows do not burn. Serve immediately.

Dan Graham Crackers

Lee Krasner Dessert Moon

Lee Krasner Dessert Moon

Makes 3 pints (1.4 l)

In Karen Holden's poem "Quartet for Desert Moon" (2013), a response to Lee Krasner's remarkable 1955 composition, she describes "a bruised red of late apples, persimmon and rose." Inspired by this synesthetic melding of vision and taste, this trio of sorbets attempts to translate the vivid intensity and jagged rhythms of Krasner's collage through the sweet fruits of the earth. It is an ode to the insurmountable task of trying to pin down an abstract feeling, the swelling emotions that comprise the delicacy and ineffable vulnerability of life.

For the simple syrup

6½ cups	(1.3 kg)	sugar

For the plum sorbet

1½ pounds	(680 g)	ripe plums (4 large plums)
2 cups	(480 ml)	simple syrup

For the raspberry sorbet

4 cups	(510 g)	raspberries
2 cups	(480 ml)	simple syrup
2–3 tbsp		fresh lemon juice
1 tsp		Crème Yvette or framboise

For the rose apple sorbet

1	pound	(454 g)	apples	(3 medium apples)
2	cups	(480 ml)	simple syrup	
1	tsp		rose water	

Steps

1   Make the simple syrup: In a saucepan, dissolve the sugar in 6½ cups (1.6 l) water over medium heat. Set aside.

2   Make the plum sorbet: Pit and dice the plums. Leave the skin on. In a saucepan, combine the plums with ¼ cup (60 ml) water and cook over medium-low heat for 5 to 10 minutes. The plums will become fragrant as they break down. Add the simple syrup and cook for an additional 1 to 2 minutes. Let cool.

3   Transfer the mixture to a blender and purée until smooth. Refrigerate until cold, then transfer to an ice-cream machine and churn. Freeze in a quart-sized (1 l) container.

4   Make the raspberry sorbet: In a saucepan, combine the raspberries with a few tablespoons of water and cook over low heat until the fruit begins to break down, a few minutes. Add the simple syrup and cook for an additional 1 to 2 minutes. Let cool.

5   Add the lemon juice and liqueur. Transfer to a blender and purée until smooth. Pass the raspberry mixture through a sieve or use a food mill to catch seeds. Refrigerate until cold, then transfer to an ice-cream machine and churn. Freeze in a quart-sized (1 l) container.

6   Make the rose apple sorbet: Core and dice the apples. Leave the skin on. In a saucepan, combine the apples with a few tablespoons of water. Cook over medium-low heat for 5 to 10 minutes. Add the simple syrup and cook for an additional 1 to 2 minutes. Stir in the rose water. Let cool.

7   Transfer to a blender and purée until smooth. Refrigerate until cold, then transfer to an ice-cream machine and churn. Freeze in a quart-sized (1 l) container.

8   Create the collage: Scoop, slice, or cut the sorbets into a variety of shapes inspired by *Desert Moon*'s biomorphic petals. Place on individual plates or a large serving platter and serve immediately.

Eva Hesse Eton Mess

Eva Hesse Eton Mess

Serves 8 to 10

Desserts, like recipes, are objects of creation based on convention. But sometimes it's nice to question why we do the things we do, why things have to look a certain way, and who sets the often arbitrary standards of perfection. Meringue is a creation based on such conventions. Despite its craggy and organic formal possibilities, few often deviate from the picture-perfect norm. Yet as a weightless, structural, and malleable substance, it can adopt different forms with ease and immediacy. Inspired by the biomorphic sculptures of Eva Hesse, who explored the sculptural possibilities hidden in elastic materials and forms, this Eton Mess takes the standard meringue, whipped cream, and berry trifecta and turns it on its head, literally. Handle the meringue in ways you had never imagined: build a surface, make a tower, apply it with a paintbrush, make it unconventional. Have the courage to let the properties of ingredients guide you to strange and exciting outcomes.

For the meringue

1¼	cups	(248 g)	granulated sugar
5			egg whites, chilled
1	tsp		rose water (optional)

1½	cups	(360 ml)	heavy cream, chilled

1	pound	(454 g)	ripe strawberries, hulled

Steps

1   Prepare the sugar: Preheat the oven to 375°F (190°C) and line a rimmed baking sheet with parchment paper. Place the sugar on the lined baking sheet and bake it for 5 minutes. Do not let it burn. Remove from the oven and reduce the temperature to 250°F (120°C).

2   Make the meringue: Using a handheld or stand mixer fitted with the whisk attachment, beat the cold egg whites until soft peaks form. Slowly add the baked sugar, 1 teaspoon at a time.

3   Once all of the sugar is added, beat the egg whites until stiff peaks form, 7 to 8 minutes. (Place an icepack under the bowl to keep the bowl chilly, which will help whip the egg whites.) Add the rose water (if using) and mix for another 30 seconds.

4   On a baking sheet lined with parchment paper, dollop the meringue into various shapes. Or use a brush to paint onto the parchment. Let the meringue's behavior guide your elastic compositions. Bake the meringue for 2½ hours, turn off the oven, then let the meringue gradually come to room temperature in the oven with the oven door ajar, for several hours, until completely cool. This will ensure a crisp texture.

5   Embrace the mess: In the bowl of a stand mixer fitted with the whisk attachment, whip the chilled heavy cream until it reaches a sensuous volume. On a large platter, begin building a sculptural creation, alternating with meringue shapes, whipped cream, and strawberries. Play with the peaks of cream and allow the strawberries to leak their syrupy goodness all over the place. Guide the creation to gravity-defying extremes. Serve within 1 hour of assembly, utensils optional.

Eva Hesse Eton Mess

Fischli and Weisscream

Fischli and Weisscream

Yields 1½ pints (0.7 l)

For art world pranksters Peter Fischli and David Weiss, anything goes:
the point is to create by embracing both order and chaos. We think the same
approach should be taken toward weisscream. Consider this canvas of sweet
vanilla custard an invitation for absurd play and humorous defacement.
Infused with a bay leaf, to give your journey toward the unusual a
herbaceous head start, treat culinary experimentation as a date with chance.
Flip a coin and observe how strange, unanticipated juxtapositions of flavor
collide when combining ordinary supermarket ingredients. Candy, meat,
fruit, and herb—it's all fair game.

2	cups	(480 ml)	heavy cream
1	cup	(240 ml)	whole milk
⅔	cup	(135 g)	granulated sugar
2			bay leaves
pinch			sea salt
6	large		egg yolks
¼	tsp		pure vanilla extract

Steps

1   In a saucepan, combine the heavy cream, milk, sugar, bay leaves, and salt over medium-low heat. Simmer until the salt and sugar dissolve, about 5 minutes. Remove the pot from the heat and let the bay leaves infuse in the liquid as the mixture cools.

2   In a medium bowl, whisk the egg yolks. While whisking, slowly add a ladle of the hot cream mixture into the egg yolks. Pour the egg mixture back into the saucepan with the remainder of the cream mixture and stir.

3   Place the saucepan on the burner and cook over medium-low heat, stirring constantly, until the mixture thickens enough to coat the back of a spoon. Strain the custard through a strainer into a bowl and stir in the vanilla. Let the mixture cool, cover, then chill in the refrigerator for at least 4 hours.

4   Transfer to an ice-cream machine and churn. At this point, you can throw in whatever flavors or ingredients you desire. You can eat right away or transfer to pint-sized containers and freeze.

Fischli and Weisscream

Richard Serradurra

Richard Serradurra

Serves 6

Originating from Macau, *serradura* (Portuguese for "sawdust") is a saccharine invention made, largely, out of industrially produced foodstuffs. Assembled like automation, the dessert comes together swiftly through actions: cranking, prying, stirring, whipping, pouring, crushing, spilling, and piling. Calling to mind Richard Serra's *Verb List* (1967–68), in which the artist catalogued eighty-four deeds in relation to twenty-four contexts that could be applied to any unspecified material, this dessert asks you to consider not only the operations you engaged in to realize its formation, but also the technological processes that amounted to the ingredients' manufacture and packaging. Further still, while the layered pudding can be presented in glass vessels, why not allow the process of gravity to unfold and do its thing? For what better way is there to serve sawdust than in freeform piles?

20–24			Maria cookies
1	cup	(240 ml)	heavy cream
1	tsp		pure vanilla extract
½	cup	(120 ml)	condensed milk
¼–½	tsp		ground cinnamon

Steps

1   Obliterate the cookies: Crush the Maria cookies by placing them in a bag and pounding them with a rolling pin. Or, pulverize them in a food processor. Observe the cookie's gradual entropic decimation into a heap of edible rubble.

Continued

2	Construct the pudding: In a medium bowl, use an electric mixer to whip the heavy cream until fluffy and suspended in mid-air. Plop the vanilla extract into the whipped cream.

3	Drizzle the condensed milk into the whipped cream gradually. Continue beating until stiff peaks form, but do not overbeat.

4	Layer the components: Dollop a layer of whipped cream on the surface of a serving platter or dish. Spread the cream into a moon. Sprinkle a thin layer of cookie sawdust. Freckle the blanket of sawdust with cinnamon. Repeat the steps above, ending with a final sprinkle of sawdust atop a cream mound. Cover and chill in the refrigerator for 2 hours.

Caesar Pelli

Caesar Pelli

Makes 1 cocktail

Inspired by an architect preoccupied with reaching dizzying new heights, this Caesar embraces the verticality of fibrous marshland leafstalks. Not merely a decorative contrivance, fresh and dried celery add a subtle herbaceous spine to this red-hot, clam-infused tomato cocktail. Its stature is increased with pickled vegetables and accoutrements that are stacked high atop a crimson liquid. An unusual Canadian concoction originally inspired by the briny savoriness of *spaghetti alle vongole*, Caesar Pelli is a celebration of the salty liquid from the clouds, in both marshlands and sea, resulting in a flavorsome treat that is at once original and unanimously satisfying.

For the rim

½	tsp	celery salt
½	tsp	garlic salt
½		lemon or lime

For the cocktail

4½	ounces	tomato juice
(135 ml)		
2	ounces	clam juice
(60 ml)		
1	tsp	agave syrup
¹⁄₁₆	tsp	celery salt
¹⁄₁₆	tsp	black pepper
¹⁄₁₆	tsp	ground cumin
¹⁄₁₆	tsp	garlic powder
½		lime, juiced

4	dashes	Worcestershire sauce
2	dashes	Tabasco or other hot sauce
1½	ounces (45 ml)	vodka
to	taste	kosher salt and black pepper
1	stalk	celery
½	tsp	grated fresh horseradish
	slice	lemon or lime
3–5		pickled vegetables

Steps

1   Rim the glass: On a small saucer, combine the celery salt and garlic salt. Moisten the rim of a tall glass with half a lemon or lime, then invert the glass onto the saucer, allowing the spices to stick to the rim.

2   Assemble the cocktail: In the glass, combine the tomato juice, clam juice, agave, spices, lime juice, sauces, and vodka. Season with salt and pepper. Stir well with a tall stalk of celery and leave the stalk in the glass. Add a few ice cubes. Top with a mound of freshly grated horseradish. Garnish the drink with a slice of lemon or lime and an assortment of pickled vegetables spiked on a long skewer.

Caesar Pelli

Lina Bo Bacardi Cocktail

Marcel Boozethaers Egg Punch

Marcel Boozethaers Egg Punch

Serves 8 to 10

Belgian artist and poet Marcel Broodthaers famously claimed he loved using eggshells in his surreal sculptures since they are "without content other than the air." This deceptively rich and boozy eggnog recipe pays tribute to his vacuole obsession by incorporating aerated egg whites and fluffy clouds of unctuous whipped cream—a cocktail that is a *pense-bête*, or reminder, through the symbolism of milk and eggs, of the poetic fragility and simplicity of new beginnings.

4	cups (960 ml)	whole milk
½	cup (100 g)	granulated sugar
4	large	eggs, separated
1	cup (240 ml)	heavy cream
3⅓	ounces (100 ml)	bourbon or dark rum (or more to taste)
1¾	ounces (50 ml)	Courvoisier cognac (or more to taste)
1	cup (60 g)	whipped cream, lightly sweetened
—		Nutmeg

Steps

1   In a saucepan, warm 2 cups of milk over low heat.

2   In a mixing bowl, whisk the sugar into the egg yolks until thick and
    pale. Gradually whisk the warm milk into the sugar-yolk mixture.

3   Return the mixture to the saucepan and cook it over low heat, stirring
    constantly, until thickened.

4   Remove the saucepan from the heat and incorporate the heavy cream.
    Chill the mixture in the refrigerator.

5   Once chilled, add the remaining milk, bourbon or rum, and cognac to
    the eggnog mixture.

6   In a separate bowl, use an electric mixer to beat the egg whites until
    soft peaks form. Gently whisk the egg whites into the eggnog, trying to
    preserve their airy texture.

7   Transfer the eggnog to a punch bowl. When serving, top each glass
    of eggnog with a dollop of whipped cream and sprinkles of freshly
    grated nutmeg.

Marcel Boozethaers Egg Punch

Odile Decquiri

Odile Decquiri

Makes 2 cocktails

Inspired by the radical individualism of French architect Odile Decq, and especially her signature love of black, this daiquiri's subtle floral sophistication is enrobed in the ebony pitch of a sweet, Cimmerian blackberry purée. Evoking roses and funereal gloom, its raven intensity is a saturnine foil for a sweet, blithesome, and sophisticated blend of fruit, citrus, and flora.

1	cup (200 g)	granulated sugar
1	cup	blackberries, plus more for garnish
2	ounces (60 ml)	white rum
½	ounce (15 ml)	fresh lime juice
¼	ounce (8 ml)	rose water
¼	ounce (8 ml)	crème Yvette
–		Lime wedges

Steps

1   Make the simple syrup: In a saucepan, combine sugar with 1 cup
    (237 ml) water and cook over medium heat, stirring until the sugar is
    dissolved and the liquid appears clear. Remove the pan from the
    heat and let the mixture cool to room temperature. Set aside 2 ounces
    (60 ml) of the simple syrup. Transfer the remaining simple syrup to
    an airtight container and store in the refrigerator for up to 1 month

2   In a blender, blend the berries and the simple syrup. Strain seeds from
    the blackberry mixture using a fine sieve, and return the blackberry
    syrup to the blender. Add the rum, lime juice, rose water, and Crème
    Yvette. Add two handfuls of ice and purée.

3   Pour into 2 glasses. Garnish with additional blackberries and lime
    wedges.

Odile Decquiri

Faith Ringgold Harlem Cocktail

Faith Ringgold Harlem Cocktail

Makes 1 cocktail

A halo of light, this golden-hued concoction inspired by artist and writer Faith Ringgold is a potion for positivity and resilience. How could a maraschino-flavored pineapple elixir not repel any clouds of despair? Based on a Harlem cocktail, a nod to the artist's birthplace, the addition of lime adds an even brighter note to this magical cordial. You'll be all smiles as you sip to celebrate the sweetness of life.

2	chunks	pineapple, about 2 inches (5 cm) long
1½	ounces (45 ml)	maraschino liqueur
1	ounce (30 ml)	pineapple juice
1	tsp	fresh lime juice
1½	ounces (45 ml)	gin

Steps

1   In a cocktail shaker, pound the pineapple and maraschino liqueur using a muddler or the end of a rolling pin.

2   Add the pineapple juice, lime juice, and gin.

3   Fill the shaker with ice, cover, and shake vigorously. Strain into a chilled glass.

Faith Ringgold Harlem Cocktail

Sterling Ruby Cocktail

Sterling Ruby Cocktail

Makes 1 cocktail

Sterling Ruby's crimson sculptures form the inspiration for this brazen cocktail, dripping in red chile spice. Monumental in flavor, its power is not to be underestimated. Smoky, tempestuous, sweet, and sour, grapefruit adds a pucker before your tongue wags from the force of its tequila punch.

2 ounces (60 ml)	chile-infused tequila
3½ ounces (100 ml)	ruby red grapefruit juice
half	lime, juiced
–	Sparkling water
–	Fresh or dried whole hot chile peppers

Steps

1   In a glass, combine the chile-infused tequila, grapefruit juice, and lime juice.

2   Add ice cubes and top with sparking water.

3   Garnish with fresh or dried hot chiles and serve.

Sterling Ruby Cocktail

Robert   Heinecken   Shandy

Robert Heinecken Shandy

Makes 1 cocktail

Self-described "paraphotographer" Robert Heinecken was interested in appropriation and found photographic imagery culled from the mass media—a world of appearances—to play with the maxim that things are not always what they seem. Likewise, the shandygaff, a nineteenth-century invention by British soldiers to ration their ale supplies, launched numerous knockoffs around the world, each with its own spin on the beer-juice combo. One such counterfeit is this recipe for a luminous and golden drink of lemon soda and beer. Consider it a work of art in the age of mixological reproduction.

¼ cup (60 ml)	fresh lemon juice (juice of 1 lemon)	
2 tsp	agave syrup	
¼ cup (60 ml)	sparkling water	
—	Beer, chilled	
slices	lemon	

Steps

1   In a glass, combine the lemon juice, agave, and sparking water.

2   Add ice cubes and top with chilled beer.

3   Garnish with lemon slices.

Acknowledgments

Like crafting an elaborate meal, a book is an exercise in perseverance and an experience in forming bonds of kinship among its participants. I am grateful to the circle of human beings that allowed this thought experiment to take shape in unexpected and serendipitous ways.

I am indebted to Holly La Due at Prestel for taking a risk on a seed, a kernel, or a crumb of an idea (really, any pun will do). It was a brave act to take on a proposal issued by a self-professed recovering academic, then-and-still unknown to the culinary world. She argued for the merits of the project and her guidance and insights were crucial to shepherding this publication into reality.

My inimitable friend, Carson Chan, is owed my gratitude for his generosity of spirit that led him to show his former college mate, Holly, an invitation for a forthcoming *Le Corbuffet* event. Ever the connector of people and ideas, his kindly disposition is what makes friendship such a rewarding and excellent ingredient of life.

I am thankful for the opportunity to collaborate with Studio Lin, whose brilliant design practice I have long admired. Witnessing Alex Lin and Jena Myung craft the book you now hold in your hands was an invaluable and thrilling learning experience.

I would also like to thank Kerry Acker for her eloquent copyediting.

Credit and appreciation must be bestowed on my parents, Miriam and Harry, and my extended family, a clan comprising a particularly diverse group of immigrants and first-generation North Americans originating from North Korea, South Korea, China, Bolivia, Canada, Barbados, and the United States. My love of food in eclectic and often incongruous combinations arose as a digestive survival tactic at our family occasions, where abundant platters of lasagna, kimchi, and mango salad shared equal real estate on the dinner table. I learned from them, through example, about food's intrinsic relationship to humor, migration, connection, and belonging.

To my beautiful crew of friends spanning several continents: Thank you for being my taste-testers, participants, and cheering squad. Your encouragement and support kept this strange experiment going.

This book is dedicated to the neighborhood of Bed Stuy, Brooklyn, a community that taught me a great deal about the pleasures and tribulations surrounding food: its diversity, its availability, its waste, and its politics. The valence of working on a cookbook while living in an area with the highest rate of child food insecurity in New York City was not lost on me.

It is also dedicated to the memory of my aunt, Adela Doyle, whose indulgent buffet tables made every gathering unforgettable. Ever the consummate host, her raucous laughter and generosity of spirit made everyone, even newcomers, feel like they were part of our family—a skill we should all aspire to hone.

Index

252, 253

Index

Index

© Prestel Verlag, Munich · London · New York 2019
A member of Verlagsgruppe Random House GmbH
Neumarkter Strasse 28 · 81673 Munich

Prestel Publishing Ltd.
14-17 Wells Street
London W1T 3PD

Prestel Publishing
900 Broadway, Suite 603
New York, NY 10003

Library of Congress Cataloging-in-Publication Data

Names: Choi, Esther, author.
Title: Le corbuffet : edible art and design classics / Esther Choi.
Other titles: Corbuffet | Edible art and design classics
Description: Munich ; London ; New York : Prestel, 2019. |
        Includes index.
Identifiers: LCCN 2019002881 | ISBN 9783791384726 (hardcover)
Subjects: LCSH: Food presentation. | Food craft. | Appropriation
        (Art) | Cooking. | LCGFT: Cookbooks.
Classification: LCC TX740.5 .C45 2019 | DDC 641.3--dc23
LC record available at https://lccn.loc.gov/2019002881

A CIP catalogue record for this book is available from the
British Library.

Editorial direction: Holly La Due
Design and layout: Studio Lin
Production: Anjali Pala
Copyediting: Kerry Acker
Proofreading: Caitlin Leffel
Index: Suzanne Fass

Verlagsgruppe Random House FSC® N001967
Printed on the FSC®-certified paper

Printed in China

ISBN 978-3-7913-8472-6

www.prestel.com